MARDI GRAS
TO
MISTLETOE

A Cookbook of Festive Favorites
from the Junior League of
Shreveport-Bossier, Louisiana

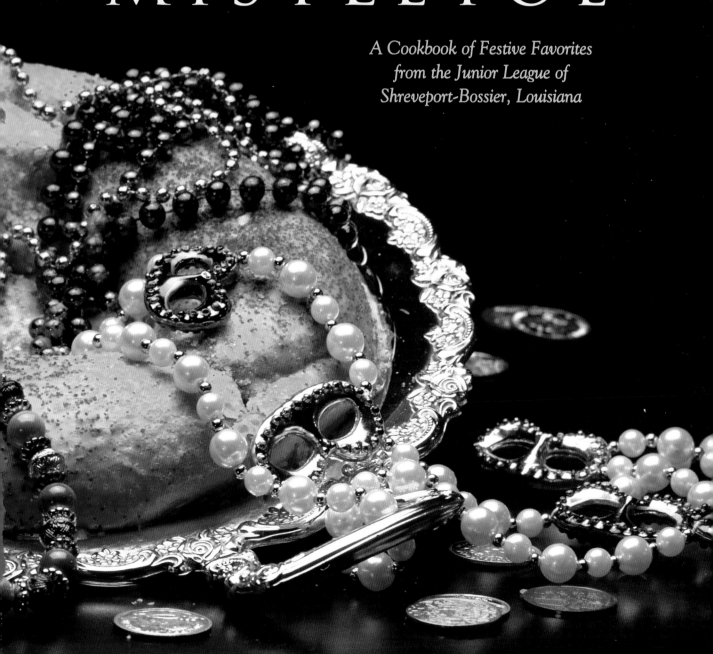

$\mathcal{M}$ARDI GRAS TO MISTLETOE

A Cookbook of Festive Favorites from the Junior League of Shreveport-Bossier, LA

Copyright © 2007

Junior League of Shreveport-Bossier, Inc.
520 Olive Street, Suite B204
Shreveport, Louisiana 71104
318-221-6144
www.jlsb.org

Photography © Neil Johnson

This cookbook is a collection of our favorite recipes,
which are not necessarily original recipes.

Library of Congress Control Number 2006922008

ISBN 0-9602246-0-2
978-0-9602246-0-9

Edited and Manufactured by **Favorite Recipes® Press**

An imprint of **FRP**

P.O. Box 305412
Nashville, Tennessee 37230
1-800-358-0560

Art Direction Steve Newman
Starletta Polster

Book Design Susan Rae Stegall

Project Editor Tanis Westbrook

Manufactured in China

First Printing 2007 10,000 copies

THANK YOU

The Junior League of Shreveport-Bossier would like
to thank the many individuals who gave of their time,
intellect, imagination, property, and services to bring
Mardi Gras to Mistletoe to reality. We hope that you
share with us in the celebration of its success and that
you are as proud of the final project as we are.
Your generous support makes this as much
yours to treasure as it is ours.

DEDICATION

This book is dedicated to all the women who volunteer in Northwest Louisiana. These ladies give unconditionally, making a difference in the lives of people every day. Their spirit of selflessness and their determination to overcome obstacles continuously create positive changes in our community. Their zest for life is found in the people and events that celebrate Northwest Louisiana today.

MISSION STATEMENT

The Association of Junior Leagues International, Inc., is an organization of women committed to promoting voluntarism, developing the potential of women, and improving communities through effective action and leadership of trained volunteers. Its purpose is exclusively educational and charitable.

VISION STATEMENT

Through the power of our association, Junior Leagues strengthen communities by embracing diverse perspectives, building partnerships, and inspiring shared solutions.

REACHING OUT STATEMENT

The Association of Junior Leagues International, Inc., reaches out to women of all races, religions, and national origins who demonstrate an interest in, and commitment to, voluntarism.

PURPOSE

Proceeds from *Mardi Gras to Mistletoe* help provide financial support for the Junior League of Shreveport-Bossier, Inc., and its mission. Since 1933, our projects have been focused on social work, helping children, and helping the needy. Today, we proudly continue our mission by concentrating our efforts on the needs of our community.

FOREWORD

• •

*I*n the aftermath of Hurricane Katrina and its destruction of New Orleans, the population of Baton Rouge almost doubled and Shreveport was surprised to find itself the second largest city in Louisiana, a state known the world over for its dining habits. With the sad and hopefully temporary loss of New Orleans, one of the food capitals of the world, Shreveport has the profound duty to step up to the plate, so to speak, and help the state of Louisiana live up to its culinary reputation, and, yes, even raise the bar locally. In my experience, it is doing just that. Take this cookbook as evidence.

They say Japanese eat with their eyes and Americans eat with their noses. This may be true, but, personally, I eat with a fork, spoon, my fingers, or whatever is put before me. I also enjoy photographing whatever is put before me. It's like a big puzzle. Assemble all the pieces and then find the best way to put them together, piece by piece, into an attractive image—foreground, food, flowers, background, lights. Prop that pheasant up. Fluff the flag a bit more. Move those beans in a bit to the right. There are myriad ways to frame each image and a shoot could go on forever, but you see here where our creative muses led us.

The capable production team and I could have gone in one of two directions with these food illustrations. The first would have been to focus on the food up tight. The second, and the one we chose, was to back off and illustrate the food *and* the settings, i.e., tablescapes. Thus, we included the food, but also some distinctly Northwestern Louisiana scenery and Junior League members' homes as backgrounds: azalea bushes in the elegant backyard of Minou Fritze, the hunt room of Judy Chidlow, the Cross Lake pier of Monica Davenport-Wesley, and the stately homes of Kim Campbell and Teresa Meldrum. Also, because we were not up close and personal with the food, we did not have to use the fine art of food styling. In other words, we avoided most of the trickery that makes food more presentable to the camera, but at the same time, inedible. Why do I mention this? Because, after we wrapped each shoot, much of the food could still be consumed . . . and consumed it was. Oh, the Grilled Tenderloin with Blueberry Sauce was delicious, as was the Streusel-Topped Pumpkin Pie, Fall Bean Salad, Shrimp Pastry Shells, and Crawfish and Corn Soup!

• •

Because one of the purposes of the Junior League is to help make this community a better place, the decision was also made to show off this community. Thus, we have interspersed images of tablescapes with images of the beauty and events that make this community wonderfully unique: things like Pumpkin Shine on Line, the Barksdale Air Force Base Air Show, Mardi Gras parades, and the spring explosion of azalea blossoms. It has been my distinct opportunity to photograph every facet of this community since the mid-1970s. Sharing these images with viewers makes the effort to create them worth it.

It should make this community proud to consider what the Junior League has accomplished, and continues to accomplish, generation after generation. This may seem like simply an attractive and helpful cookbook, but if you look closely and breathe deeply, you will realize it has been carefully and lovingly marinated with the message and goals of the Junior League of Shreveport-Bossier. It is my hope that this cookbook will inspire cooks throughout this corner of the state, and far outside it, to continue the culinary traditions of Louisiana and to instill in its users a continuing pride in Northwest Louisiana and the Junior League.

I am not now, nor have I ever been, a Junior Leaguer, but I am so proud to have been called upon to collaborate on this project with these happy few—this band of sisters.

Neil Johnson

PREFACE

*S*ince the 1940s, Junior Leagues from across the nation have been raising funds with their cookbooks. The Junior League of Minneapolis published the first one in 1943. By the 1950s, Junior League cookbooks were recognized as key fund-raising tools throughout the organization. Presently, there are more than two hundred such cookbooks in print, raising funds for the various Leagues and their community projects.

The Junior League of Shreveport-Bossier began its cookbook fund-raising with *A Cook's Tour* in 1964. The success of this cookbook and the introduction of the Red River Revel Arts Festival prompted the publishing of the *Revel* cookbook in 1979. Now, in the new millennium, we are proud to present our new cookbook, *Mardi Gras to Mistletoe*.

Every detail of this cookbook has been lovingly prepared by the ever-dedicated 2005–2006 cookbook committee; however, making it worthy to follow in the footsteps of the incredibly popular cookbooks before it was no easy feat. As the title and theme suggest, *Mardi Gras to Mistletoe* pays tribute to the festivals and traditions celebrated by the people of Northwest Louisiana. League members, their families, and favorite local restaurants donated recipes, which were then tirelessly tested to make sure they were as easy to prepare as they were tasty. To complement the festive recipes, a talented and well-known local photographer, Neil Johnson, was recruited to bring visual flair to the cookbook. Finally, months of research and editing tied it all together.

Each of the twelve chapters highlights a particular month of the year and begins with a brief narrative of the history, festivals, and traditions celebrated in that month. The chapters are then filled with recipes that can be used to create a seasonal menu or a stand-alone special dish. We hope this cookbook will entice readers to try all of the recipes when planning successful celebrations of their own.

The Junior League of Shreveport-Bossier invites you to read with us, cook with us, and celebrate with us . . . Northwest Louisiana style!

COOKBOOK COMMITTEE

COOKBOOK EXECUTIVE COMMITTEE

Martha Siskron
Chairman

Imelda Torres
Assistant Chairman

Kay deBerardinis
President

Ginger Lukacs
President-elect

COOKBOOK COMMITTEE

Cris Bregman	Carolyn Sharpe
Jessica Bretz	Shannon Slatton
Heather Conly	Nadean Tanner
Tara Johnston	Farris Todd
Teresa LeBleu	Kendra Wheeler

PHOTOGRAPHY/DESIGN SET-UP

Brooke Benson	Teresa LeBleu
Jessica Bretz	Suzy Littlejohn
Kay deBerardinis	Lona Lockard
Michelle Hardtner	Ginger Lukacs
Wendy Harper	Lucy Medvec
Pat Hendrick	Libby Siskron
Allyson Lawson	Martha Siskron

CELEBRATED HOMES

Mr. & Mrs. Chip Campbell page 13   Mr. & Mrs. Patrick Wesley page 111
Mr. & Mrs. George Fritze page 45   Dr. & Mrs. Judd Chidlow page 173
Mr. & Mrs. John Meldrum page 75

CELEBRATED LANDSCAPES

Mardi Gras Parade in Shreveport page 29

Azaleas at the Norton Art Gallery page 61

Sunflowers in Giliam page 93

Texas Street Bridge over the Red River page 125

Pumpkin Shine on Line page 159

Natchitoches Light Festival page 189

Contents

Introduction 10

JANUARY 11

FEBRUARY 27

MARCH 43

APRIL 59

MAY 73

JUNE 91

JULY 109

AUGUST 123

SEPTEMBER 139

OCTOBER 157

NOVEMBER 171

DECEMBER 187

Contributors 200

Index 202

Order Information 208

INTRODUCTION

*W*hether you were born in Northwest Louisiana, transplanted from somewhere else, or are just a visitor passing through, you will most likely notice that there's something special about our area. While you may not be able to put your finger on it, you will probably agree that it's a good thing. Few things define the culture of a region like its festivals and food, and that is exactly what we have attempted to capture in the pages of *Mardi Gras to Mistletoe*. This cookbook is a collection of favorite recipes intermingled with the time-honored festivals and celebrations that represent the traditions and soul of our home.

The sister cities of Shreveport and Bossier City are the cultural and economic anchors of Northwest Louisiana. The port cities, which are located in the extreme northwest corner of the state, are separated by the Red River. Smaller cities across the region add flavor and diversity. Former boom-towns Blanchard, Oil City, Benton, and Vivian dot the north, while the rich cultural areas of Stonewall, Mansfield, Zwolle, and Natchitoches extend to central Louisiana. The communities of Minden, Gibsland, and Ruston are to the east, and Greenwood nestles the Texas border to the west. The more well-known cities of New Orleans and Baton Rouge may shine to the far south, but the cities and people of Northwest Louisiana definitely have a style all their own. And what a beautifully rich and colorful style it is!

The name Louisiana rolls off the tongue with a lilt that tickles the soul and conjures up images of a unique and fascinating culture and lifestyle well known for its deep, fun-loving French-Creole influence. The heritage of the people of the Northwest portion of the state make up a rich cultural gumbo, which includes early American pioneers, African Americans, French Canadian exiles, European settlers, Native Americans, and many others. With this mixture, it's no wonder that the people, traditions, and festivals of modern-day Northwest Louisiana are also so unique and colorful.

Communities first developed in this part of the state nearly two centuries ago. The earliest settlers established themselves largely in Natchitoches, Webster, and Claiborne parishes to the south and east of current Shreveport. These early pioneers initially shared the land with the Caddo Indians, and their communities thrived largely on the logging and cotton industries. The clearing of the "Red River Raft," or "great log jam" as it has also come to be known, was the most significant factor in the growth of the area. This great raft of debris had blocked the river for hundreds of years and stretched from bank to bank for a length of more than 150 miles, extending from Fulton, Arkansas, to Natchitoches, Louisiana. River engineer Captain Henry M. Shreve accepted the challenge to clear the raft, and on April 1, 1833, work began to make the Red River a vital artery of commerce. *Captain Shreve never called the city that bears his name home, but his contribution continues to make the river an important part of the economy.*

Northwest Louisiana likes to celebrate, and you can find a festival in honor of almost anything, from flowers indigenous to the region to the fruits and vegetables harvested in the area. You can also attend festivals that honor the people who have contributed to the culture and history of Northwest Louisiana, ranging from the famous, such as guitarist James Burton, to the infamous, such as Bonnie and Clyde. There is no denying, though, that food always seems to be the center of any Northwest Louisiana celebration.

It is our goal to provide you with recipes that will make any meal a celebration and any celebration a success. Whether you are toasting at the most elegant event or stomping your feet with the rowdiest of tailgaters, these recipes will arm you with dishes that are not only delicious but also so easy to prepare that the host will be able to get out of the kitchen and have a good time, too.

So pick your next event—a birthday, a graduation, or maybe a gathering of friends "just because." No matter what you plan to celebrate, let the Junior League of Shreveport-Bossier and *Mardi Gras to Mistletoe* help you capture what makes Northwest Louisiana so special. Capture it, savor it, and pass it on to generations to come.

JANUARY

The celebration and anticipation of good things

to come that herald the month of January are

new year's

hard to match in any other month of the year.

twelfth night celebration

Whether the month begins with a kiss at

midnight or a brilliant fireworks display, it

always marks a perfect time for a fresh start.

*T*he celebration of the New Year is one of the oldest known to civilization, with the earliest observance believed to have been around 2000 B.C. Its observance on January 1st, however, is a relatively new tradition, first introduced by Julius Caesar in 46 B.C. when he added January and February to the Roman calendar. All around the world, people celebrate the coming of the NEW YEAR with traditions handed down over the centuries to either purge the "evils" of the past year or bring good luck and fortune in the new one.

Traditionally, it was thought that one could affect the luck they would have in the coming year by what they did, who they first met, or what they ate on the first day of the year. For that reason, it has become common to celebrate the first few minutes of a new year in the company of family, friends, and plenty of good food. Many choose to gather to drink champagne, sing "Auld Lang Syne," and kiss that special someone as the clock strikes midnight. Some fun lovers gather to shoot fireworks or watch the crystal ball drop at the Times Square New Year's Eve celebration, an American tradition since 1907. Another favorite American New Year's tradition, dating back to 1890, is watching the Tournament of Roses Parade and the Rose Bowl football game that soon follows. Whatever the choice of celebration, though, there is no denying that people like to begin the year together, and food is frequently part of the celebration.

Probably the most famous Southern culinary New Year's tradition is eating black-eyed peas and ham hocks, and this holds true in Northwest Louisiana, too. Black-eyed peas are considered good luck in many cultures, and the hog has long been considered lucky because owning one was a symbol of prosperity. Cabbage is another "good luck" vegetable consumed on New Year's Day by many in this area. Its leaves represent paper currency, and thus, prosperity.

In Northwest Louisiana, while the cheerful memories of our New Year's celebrations still linger, we celebrate again with the Krewes of Gemini and Centaur and their annual TWELFTH NIGHT CELEBRATION. This marks the official beginning of the Mardi Gras season in the Shreveport-Bossier area, and all local Krewes are invited to the party to present their royalty. The Mardi Gras revelers begin their festivities toasting with flutes filled with champagne to warm the spirit. Party trays heavily laden with delicious and unique delicacies help to keep the celebrations flavorful.

With the coming of the New Year, some may look back and reminisce about the days gone by, while others are inspired to make a fresh start with resolutions to make changes for the better. January is when it all begins, and in Northwest Louisiana January begins all the fun.

VODKA SNOW

The drink will have the effect of ice and snow.

Serves 6 to 8

ingredients

1½ cups sugar

Grated zest and juice of 2 small
    lemons or 1 large lemon

2 teaspoons lemon extract

1 cup half-and-half

Vodka (optional)

1 (2-liter) bottle lemon-lime soda

method

Combine the sugar, lemon zest, lemon juice and flavoring in a pitcher and whisk until combined. Stir in the half-and-half. Chill, covered, in the refrigerator.

To serve, pour 1 shot glass of the chilled lemon mixture and 1 shot glass of vodka over crushed ice in a glass. Add enough of the soda to fill the glass and serve immediately.

CHAMPAGNE SORBET*

Serves 10 to 12

ingredients

2 cups sugar

1 cup water

1 teaspoon egg white

1 teaspoon light corn syrup

3 cups Champagne

2 cups orange pineapple juice

*Photograph for this recipe on page 13.

method

Combine the sugar and water in a small saucepan and stir until the sugar dissolves. Bring the mixture to a boil and remove from the heat. Let stand until cool.

Whisk the egg white and corn syrup in a bowl until blended. Stir in 1¼ cups of the cooled sugar syrup, the Champagne and juice. Pour the Champagne mixture into an ice cream freezer container and freeze using the manufacturer's directions. Use the remaining sugar syrup for another batch of sorbet. If you are concerned about using raw egg whites, use eggs pasteurized in their shells, which are sold at some specialty food stores, or use an equivalent amount of pasteurized egg substitute.

SHRIMP PASTRY SHELLS*

Makes 30

ingredients

1 cup sour cream
8 ounces cream cheese, softened
   and cubed
1 envelope ranch dip mix
1 (4-ounce) can shrimp, drained
   and chopped
1 (3-ounce) jar bacon pieces
30 frozen phyllo shells
30 deveined peeled boiled shrimp
Chopped fresh chives

*Photograph for this recipe on page 13.

method

Combine the sour cream and cream cheese in a saucepan and cook over low heat until smooth, stirring frequently. Add the dip mix and stir until blended. Remove from the heat and stir in the canned shrimp and 1 tablespoon of the bacon. Let cool slightly.

Spoon about 1 teaspoon of the cream cheese mixture into each phyllo shell and top each with 1 boiled shrimp. Sprinkle with the remaining bacon and chives.

NOTE: *Reduce the fat grams by using fat-free sour cream, fat-free cream cheese and fat-free ranch dip mix. Fresh cooked shrimp may be substituted for the canned shrimp, if desired.*

ASPARAGUS PARTY ROLLS*

Makes 40 rolls

ingredients

1 loaf extra-thin white bread or
   whole wheat bread
8 ounces cream cheese, softened
3 ounces blue cheese
1 egg, lightly beaten
2 (15-ounce) cans asparagus
   spears, drained
1/2 cup (1 stick) butter, melted

*Photograph for this recipe on page 13.

method

Trim the crusts from the bread slices and flatten with a rolling pin. Mix the cream cheese, blue cheese and egg in a bowl until blended and spread over one side of each bread slice. Arrange 1 asparagus spear on each prepared bread slice and roll up. Secure each roll with three wooden picks.

Dip the rolls in the melted butter and arrange on a baking sheet. Freeze until firm and store in a sealable plastic bag in the freezer. To serve, thaw the number of rolls desired in the refrigerator and arrange on a baking sheet. Bake at 400 degrees for 15 minutes or until light brown. Serve as is or cut each roll into three bite-size pieces.

JACK QUESADILLAS WITH CRANBERRY PEAR RELISH*

Makes 8 quesadillas

*Photograph for this recipe on page 13.

ingredients

CRANBERRY PEAR RELISH
1 cup whole cranberry sauce
1 Anjou pear, finely chopped
1 jalapeño chile, seeded and minced
2 tablespoons chopped green onions
1 tablespoon fresh lime juice
1/2 teaspoon ground cumin

QUESADILLAS
8 (8-inch) flour tortillas
1 cup (4 ounces) shredded Pepper
   Jack cheese
2 cups chopped cooked turkey
   or chicken
Sour cream

method

RELISH
Combine the cranberry sauce, pear, jalapeño chile, green onions, lime juice and cumin in a bowl and mix well. Chill, covered, in the refrigerator.

QUESADILLAS
Layer each of four tortillas with 2 tablespoons of the cheese and 1/2 cup of the turkey. Sprinkle each with 2 tablespoons of the remaining cheese and top each with one of the remaining tortillas.

Heat a large nonstick skillet over medium-high heat and spray with nonstick cooking spray. Cook the quesadillas one at a time for 2 minutes per side or until the tortilla is light brown and the cheese melts. Cut each quesadilla into six wedges and serve with the relish and sour cream.

OLIVE CHEESE PUFFS*

Makes 4 dozen puffs

ingredients

8 ounces Cheddar cheese, shredded
1 1/4 cups all-purpose flour
1/2 cup (1 stick) butter, melted
1/2 teaspoon Cajun seasoning
1 (13-ounce) jar pimento-stuffed
   green olives, drained

*Photograph for this recipe on page 13.

method

Mix the cheese and flour in a bowl until crumbly and stir in the butter and Cajun seasoning. Pat the olives dry with paper towels. Enclose each olive in 1 teaspoon of the dough.

Arrange the olive balls on a baking sheet and bake at 400 degrees for 15 to 20 minutes or until light brown. For variety, use jalapeño chile-stuffed olives or garlic-stuffed olives.

DERBY CHEESE TORTA*

Serves 15 to 20

1 (10-ounce) package frozen
   chopped spinach, thawed
   and drained
12 ounces sharp Cheddar cheese,
   shredded
1 cup pecan pieces
1/2 onion, chopped
16 ounces cream cheese, softened
1/2 cup chutney, such as Major
   Grey's mango chutney
1 tablespoon beef bouillon granules
1/4 teaspoon garlic salt
1/8 teaspoon oregano
1/8 teaspoon basil

*Photograph for this recipe on page 13.

Press the excess moisture from the spinach and chop. Combine the Cheddar cheese, pecans and onion in a bowl and mix well. Spread one-half of the Cheddar cheese mixture in an 8-inch springform pan. Mix 8 ounces of the cream cheese and the chutney in a bowl and spread over the prepared layer. Combine the spinach, remaining 8 ounces cream cheese, the bouillon granules, garlic salt, oregano and basil in a bowl and mix well. Spread the spinach mixture over the prepared layers and sprinkle with the remaining Cheddar cheese mixture. Chill, covered, until serving time. Serve with assorted party crackers. For a 9- or 10-inch springform pan, increase the recipe by one-half.

NOTE: *This torta may be frozen in the pan for up to one month. Once it is frozen, remove the side and bottom of the pan and wrap the torta first in plastic wrap and then in foil. Store in the freezer for future use.*

*F*or **Holiday Cucumber Cups,** create decorative stripes on the sides of 6 cucumbers using a vegetable peeler for wide stripes or a citrus zester for thin stripes. Cut the cucumbers crosswise into 3/4-inch rounds. Using a teaspoon or melon baller, scoop out the seeds in each round to form a cup approximately 1/3 inch deep. Spoon about 1 1/2 teaspoons of red pepper hummus into each cup of half of the cucumber rounds and 1 1/2 teaspoons of lemon hummus into the remaining cups, mounding the hummus slightly. Sprinkle with chopped fresh chives. For a fancier look, use a pastry bag fitted with a large star tip to fill the cups.

Photograph for this recipe on page 13.

BLACK-EYED PEA DIP

Serves 15 to 20

ingredients

1/2 cup (1 stick) butter

1 roll garlic cheese, chopped

6 ounces Mexican Velveeta cheese, or 1 (6-ounce) roll garlic cheese spread

2 (15-ounce) cans black-eyed peas with jalapeño chiles, drained

1/2 white onion or equivalent amount of green onions, chopped

4 garlic cloves, minced

method

Heat the butter, garlic cheese and Velveeta cheese in a saucepan over low heat until blended, stirring frequently. Stir in the black-eyed peas, onion and garlic. Process the black-eyed pea mixture in a blender until puréed.

Return the purée to the saucepan and cook over low heat just until heated through, stirring occasionally. Serve warm with assorted chips. You may substitute a mixture of 2 cans of black-eyed peas and 2 tablespoons chopped jalapeño chiles for the black-eyed peas with jalapeño chiles.

GOOD LUCK SALAD*

Serves 4 to 6

ingredients

2 tablespoons red wine vinegar

2 teaspoons hot sauce

1 1/2 teaspoons canola oil

1 garlic clove, minced

1/8 teaspoon pepper

1 firm avocado, cut into 1/2-inch pieces

8 ounces Roma tomatoes, coarsely chopped

1 (15-ounce) can black-eyed peas, drained and rinsed

1 (15-ounce) can black beans, drained and rinsed

1 (11-ounce) can corn, drained

2/3 cup thinly sliced green onions

Salt to taste

*Photograph for this recipe on page 13.

method

Mix the vinegar, hot sauce, canola oil, garlic and pepper in a bowl. Add the avocado to the vinegar mixture and toss gently to coat. Stir in the tomatoes, black-eyed peas, beans, corn and green onions and season with salt. Serve on lettuce-lined salad plates or with tortilla chips.

SWEET-AND-SOUR LEEKS

This rich side dish tastes great over mashed potatoes.

Serves 4

ingredients

6 tablespoons butter
1 pound leek bulbs
2 tablespoons dark brown sugar
1/4 cup red wine vinegar
1/2 cup chicken broth
Salt and pepper to taste

method

Melt the butter in a large skillet and add the leeks. Cook, covered, over low heat for 20 minutes or until tender, stirring occasionally. Stir in the brown sugar, vinegar and broth and bring to a boil. Reduce the heat to low.

Simmer, covered, for 12 to 15 minutes or until the liquid is absorbed, stirring occasionally. Season with salt and pepper.

BAKED BLACK OLIVE MINESTRONE

Makes 31/2 quarts

ingredients

1 1/2 pounds lean beef stew meat,
   cut into 1 1/2-inch cubes
1 cup chopped onion
1 teaspoon minced garlic
1 teaspoon salt
1/4 teaspoon pepper
2 tablespoons olive oil
3 (14-ounce) cans beef broth
4 cups water
1 1/2 teaspoons Italian herb
   seasoning
1 (16-ounce) can tomatoes
1 (15-ounce) can kidney beans
1 cup small shell pasta
1 (6-ounce) can pitted black olives,
   drained
2 cups sliced zucchini
1 1/2 cups sliced carrots
Grated Parmesan cheese

method

Combine the stew meat, onion, garlic, salt and pepper in a Dutch oven or heavy ovenproof saucepan and mix well. Add the olive oil and stir until the beef is coated. Brown in a 400-degree oven for 40 minutes, stirring once or twice. Reduce the oven temperature to 350 degrees and stir in the broth, water and Italian seasoning.

Bake, covered, for 1 hour or until the beef is almost tender. Stir in the undrained tomatoes, undrained beans, pasta, olives, zucchini and carrots. Bake, covered, for 40 to 45 minutes longer or until the pasta is tender. Serve with Parmesan cheese.

BROCCOLI SAUSAGE PIE

This pie is a real man-pleaser.
Serves 12

ingredients

4 refrigerator pie crusts
2 pounds spicy sausage
1 white onion, chopped
1/2 green bell pepper, chopped
3 garlic cloves, minced
1 1/2 teaspoons salt
1/2 teaspoon pepper
4 drops of Tabasco sauce
16 ounces cream cheese, softened
1 (6-ounce) jar mushrooms, drained
1 (16-ounce) package frozen
   broccoli, cooked and drained
12 ounces mozzarella
   cheese, shredded

method

Fit one of the pie crusts into each of two 9-inch pie plates and bake using the package directions.

Cook the sausage, onion and bell pepper in a skillet, stirring until the sausage is crumbly and the vegetables are tender; drain. Stir in the garlic, salt, pepper and Tabasco sauce. Fold in the cream cheese and mushrooms. Stir in the broccoli and mozzarella cheese.

Spoon the sausage mixture evenly into the baked pie shells and top with the remaining pie crusts, fluting the edges and cutting vents. Bake at 350 degrees for 20 minutes and cover with foil. Bake for 20 minutes longer. This pie freezes beautifully. Just skip the last 20 minutes of baking before freezing.

NOTE: *To make this a lighter dish, use turkey sausage and substitute Neufchâtel cheese for the cream cheese.*

The area of Bossier City dates back to the 1830s, when it was the Elysian Groves Plantation of James and Mary Cane, whose home was located at the foot of the Texas Street bridge. Steamboat loads of cotton, corn, and sweet potatoes were shipped to markets in the south and east, from the plantation port known to many as "Cane's Landing."

CHICKEN AND SAUSAGE GUMBO

Serves 30

ingredients

2 chickens

4 chicken breasts

2 (12-ounce) cans chicken broth

5 onions, chopped

4 bell peppers, chopped

5 ribs celery, chopped

1/2 jar roux

2 pounds andouille, sliced

5 bay leaves

1/4 cup Tony Chachere's Creole
   seasoning

3 tablespoons minced garlic

1 tablespoon salt

1 tablespoon Tabasco sauce

1 teaspoon cayenne pepper

1/2 teaspoon black pepper

1/2 teaspoon thyme

method

Place the chicken in a stockpot and add enough water to fill halfway. Bring to a boil and boil until the chicken is cooked through. Remove the chicken to a platter and cool slightly. Reserve the broth in the stockpot. Shred the chicken, discarding the skin and bones. Return the chicken to the stockpot and stir in the canned broth, onions, bell peppers and celery.

Bring to a boil and boil until the vegetables are tender, stirring occasionally. Add the roux and stir until dissolved. Stir in the sausage, bay leaves, Creole seasoning, garlic, salt, Tabasco sauce, cayenne pepper, black pepper and thyme. Simmer for 30 minutes, stirring occasionally. Discard the bay leaves and ladle the gumbo into bowls. You may freeze for future use.

HEAVENLY CHICKEN CASSEROLE

Serves 10

ingredients

1 (4-ounce) package wild rice
1/2 cup (1 stick) butter or margarine
1/2 cup chopped onion
1/2 cup chopped green bell pepper
1/2 cup chopped celery
1 (10-ounce) can cream of
    mushroom soup
1 (10-ounce) can cream of
    chicken soup
4 cups chopped cooked chicken
2 cups (8 ounces) shredded
    Cheddar cheese, divided
1/2 cup sliced almonds, toasted
1 (4-ounce) jar chopped
    pimentos, drained
1 (4-ounce) can sliced
    mushrooms, drained
Salt and pepper to taste

method

Cook the rice using the package directions until almost tender and drain. Melt the butter in a Dutch oven and add the onion, bell pepper and celery. Cook until tender and remove from the heat. Stir in the soups, chicken, cooked rice, 1 1/2 cups cheese, almonds, pimentos and mushrooms. Season with salt and pepper.

Spoon the chicken mixture into a greased 9×13-inch baking dish and bake at 350 degrees for 20 minutes. Sprinkle with the remaining 1/2 cup cheese and bake for 10 to 15 minutes longer or until brown and bubbly.

On October 17, 1930, in the St. Mark's Parish House, ninety-eight young Shreveport women heard the reading of a proposed constitution and bylaws of the Junior Service League, which became the Junior League of Shreveport, Inc., three years later. With the help of the organization that would eventually become the United Way, the Junior Service League was accepted, on its first application, into the Association of Junior Leagues of America in February 1933.

CHOCOLATE AMARETTO CHEESECAKE*

· ·

Serves 8 to 12

ingredients

CHOCOLATE WAFER CRUST
1 cup chocolate wafer crumbs
1/4 cup (1/2 stick) butter, melted

CHOCOLATE AMARETTO
    FILLING
2 cups (12 ounces) chocolate chips
2 tablespoons milk
24 ounces cream cheese, softened
1 cup sour cream
3/4 cup sugar
1/2 cup amaretto
3 eggs
2 teaspoons vanilla extract

*Photograph for this recipe on page 13.

method

CRUST
Mix the wafer crumbs and butter in a bowl until combined. Press the crumb mixture over the bottom of a 9-inch springform pan.

FILLING
Heat the chocolate chips and milk in a double boiler or in the microwave until blended, stirring occasionally. Combine the cream cheese, sour cream, sugar, amaretto, eggs and vanilla in a mixing bowl and beat until smooth, scraping the bowl occasionally. Fold in the melted chocolate mixture and spread over the prepared crust. Bake at 350 degrees for 45 minutes. Cool in the pan on a wire rack. Remove the side of the pan and store the cheesecake, covered, in the refrigerator. Garnish with shaved chocolate and/or whipped cream just before serving.

MABRY HOUSE WHITE AND DARK CHOCOLATE TORTE

Serves 8 to 10

ingredients

CHOCOLATE COOKIE CRUST
3/4 package chocolate
    sandwich cookies
6 tablespoons butter, melted

CHOCOLATE FILLING
3 1/2 ounces white chocolate
6 tablespoons unsalted butter
1/4 cup heavy cream
3 1/2 ounces dark
    semisweet chocolate
6 tablespoons unsalted butter
1/4 cup heavy cream
1 3/4 cups packed brown sugar
3/4 cup all-purpose flour
6 eggs

method

CRUST
Process the cookies in a food processor until finely ground. Add the butter and process until the mixture adheres. Pat the crumb mixture into a torte pan and chill.

FILLING
Heat the white chocolate, 6 tablespoons butter and 1/4 cup heavy cream in a double boiler over simmering water until blended, whisking occasionally. Melt the semisweet chocolate and 6 tablespoons butter with 1/4 cup heavy cream in a double boiler over simmering water, whisking occasionally until blended.

Beat the brown sugar, flour and eggs in a mixing bowl until smooth. Add one-half of the brown sugar mixture to the white chocolate mixture and mix well. Stir the remaining brown sugar mixture into the semisweet chocolate mixture and mix well. Pour the white chocolate mixture and semisweet chocolate mixture over the chilled crust and swirl with a knife to mix slightly. Bake at 375 degrees for 55 minutes or until the center is set.

The Mabry House was built in 1902 by William Alexander Mabry and his wife, Nellie Lake Mabry. The house is listed on the National Register of historic places by virtue of its inclusion in the Highland Historic District. Steve and Ginger Mylar now own the house and have turned it into an upscale restaurant.

AMBROSIA BARS*

* *

This is a nice alternative to lemon bars.
Makes 2 dozen bars

ingredients

ALMOND CRUST
1¹/₄ cups all-purpose flour
¹/₂ cup finely chopped
   slivered almonds
¹/₂ cup packed brown sugar
¹/₄ teaspoon salt
1 cup (2 sticks) unsalted butter,
   chilled and cut into pieces

COCONUT FILLING
1¹/₂ cups sweetened flaked coconut
2 cups granulated sugar
¹/₂ cup orange pineapple juice
¹/₄ cup all-purpose flour
4 eggs
Confectioners' sugar to taste

*Photograph for this recipe on page 13.

method

CRUST
Line a 9×13-inch baking pan with foil, allowing for an overhang over the short sides. Mix the flour, almonds, brown sugar and salt in a bowl. Cut the butter into the flour mixture with a fork until crumbly. Dust hands lightly with flour and pat the crumb mixture over the bottom of the prepared pan. Bake at 350 degrees for 20 minutes or until the edges begin to brown. Cool in the pan on a wire rack. Maintain the oven temperature.

FILLING
Sprinkle one-half of the coconut over the baked layer. Whisk the granulated sugar, juice, flour and eggs in a bowl until blended and pour over the prepared layers. Sprinkle with the remaining coconut and bake for 30 minutes or until the top is set. Cool in the pan on a wire rack. Chill in the refrigerator. Run a knife around the edges of the baked layer to loosen. Use the foil to remove from the pan. Dust with confectioners' sugar and cut into bars.

GERMAN CHOCOLATE FONDUE*

Delicious and oh so easy to make.
Makes 2 cups

ingredients

2/3 cup light corn syrup
1/2 cup heavy cream or fat-free
   half-and-half
8 ounces German's sweet
   chocolate, chopped

*Photograph for this recipe on page 13.

method

Combine the corn syrup and heavy cream in a microwave-safe bowl and mix well. Microwave, covered, on High for 2 to 2$^{1}/_{2}$ minutes or until the mixture comes to a boil, stirring twice. Add the chocolate and stir until melted and blended. Pour the chocolate mixture into a fondue pot and serve with chunks of assorted fresh fruit.

The Caddo-Bossier Association for Retarded Children (C-BARC) occupation center was adopted as a Junior League project in 1956 to provide evaluation of training facilities and services for individuals capable of being placed in the community as self-supporting citizens. The Junior League, with the help of matching federal funds, provided training, job placement, and social contact for people between the ages of sixteen to thirty-six until C-BARC was assumed by others in the community and eventually became a United Way agency.

FEBRUARY

Our New Year's resolutions and good intentions

are tested early in the year as Mardi Gras and

mardi gras

Valentine's Day bring raucous celebration and sweet

black history month

temptation to Northwest Louisiana in February.

valentine's day

Though cold is a relative term in Louisiana, February is one of our coldest months, but that doesn't keep the celebrations inside. People line the streets by the thousands for a chance to shout, "Throw me something, Mister!" in hopes of catching more beads than can possibly be carried home.

Although the precise origins of Mardi Gras are debatable, the history of similar celebrations existed as early as the second century, when the ancient Romans observed a period in mid-February that was in many respects very similar to the present-day MARDI GRAS. In French, *Mardi Gras* literally means "Fat Tuesday," so named because it falls on the day before Ash Wednesday. This day marks the beginning of the season of Lent, a forty-day period of spiritual discipline, fasting, and moderation in preparation for Holy Week and Easter. In ancient times, Mardi Gras and the period before it beginning on the twelfth day of Christmas—January 6th—became a time of abandon and merriment, when nearly all aspects of pleasure were allowed as people prepared to forego earthly pleasures until Easter.

Mardi Gras has been celebrated as a major holiday in Paris since the Middle Ages, and it is generally accepted that the French explorer Sieur d'Iberville introduced it to Louisiana in 1699 when he camped for the holiday on the bank of the Mississippi River about sixty miles south of present-day New Orleans. By the mid-1800s, the celebrations in New Orleans became more elaborate, culminating in an annual Mardi Gras Ball.

Traditionally, Mardi Gras had little place in the more Protestant North Louisiana, but in recent years, thanks to the irresistible influence of our carnival-loving neighbors to the south, the festival has expanded its traditional boundaries. More than a dozen Mardi Gras Krewes now call the area home, and parades as spirited as any found in New Orleans are now found right in our own backyards. The most notable and favorite in the area are the parades of the Krewes of Centaur, Gemini, and Highland in Shreveport, Akewa in Minden, and Dionysos in Natchitoches. In addition to having fun, several Krewes focus on supporting charitable endeavors, including the Krewe of Barkus and Meoux, dedicated to helping abused and neglected animals; the Krewe of Harambee, with a goal to increase minority participation in and support of the Sickle Cell Anemia Foundation; and the Krewe of Sobek, whose members give back to the community through charitable donations and community service.

This month may be dominated by Mardi Gras, but don't get partied out just yet. February also marks BLACK HISTORY MONTH, an annual four-week-long celebration of African American history that has existed since 1926. And, of course, keep your hearts open to the time-honored traditions of VALENTINE'S DAY, when treats and sweets are plentiful and Cupid's arrows fill the air.

All month long the people of Northwest Louisiana celebrate their unique culture and traditions with food at the center of it all. Whether for fun or for love, it's hard to resist the tantalizing tastes that February brings.

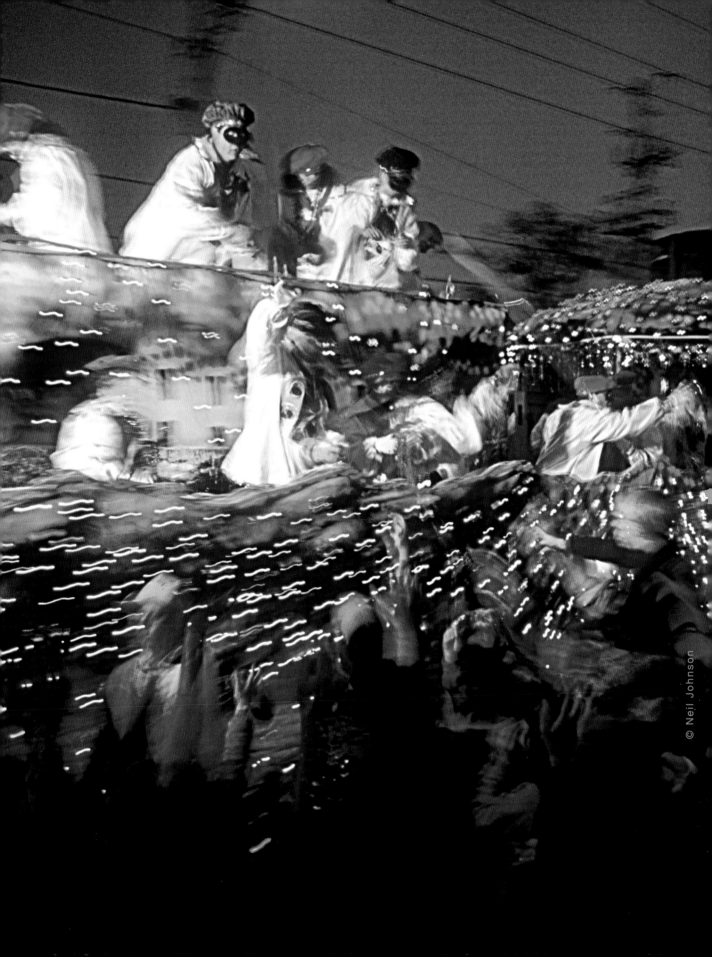

COFFEE PUNCH

Serves 40

ingredients

5 tablespoons instant
   coffee granules
6 cups cold water
2 cups hot water
1 cup sugar (optional)
3/4 cup rum (optional)
1/2 teaspoon salt
1/2 teaspoon almond flavoring
1/2 gallon vanilla ice cream
1/2 gallon chocolate ice cream
2 cups half-and-half

method

Combine the coffee granules, cold water, hot water, sugar, rum, salt and flavoring in a 1/2 gallon container and mix well. Chill for 8 to 10 hours, stirring occasionally.

Pour the coffee mixture into a punch bowl 20 minutes before serving. Add the vanilla ice cream, chocolate ice cream and half-and-half and stir until slushy. Ladle into punch cups. The sugar is optional because the punch is sweet with the ice cream alone.

MARINATED CRAB CLAWS

Serves 4 to 6

ingredients

1 pound steamed crab claws
3/4 cup extra-virgin olive oil
1/4 cup wine vinegar
1 tablespoon lemon juice
1 teaspoon salt
1 teaspoon pepper
1 teaspoon paprika
1 teaspoon Zatarain's mustard
1/2 teaspoon dry mustard
1/16 teaspoon oregano
1/2 cup chopped fresh parsley
1/4 cup finely chopped celery
3 green onions, finely chopped
1 tablespoon drained capers, rinsed
   and chopped

method

Place the crab claws in a shallow dish with a cover. Combine the olive oil, vinegar, lemon juice, salt, pepper, paprika, Zatarain's mustard, dry mustard and oregano in a bowl and mix well. Stir in the parsley, celery, green onions and capers. Pour the olive oil mixture over the crab claws and turn to coat.

Marinate, tightly covered, in the refrigerator for 2 to 10 hours, shaking the container and turning every few hours. Serve chilled with French bread to soak up the delicious marinade.

LAYERED CRAB MEAT SPREAD

Serves 12 to 15

ingredients

8 ounces cream cheese, softened
2 tablespoons lemon juice
1 tablespoon mayonnaise
1/4 teaspoon Worcestershire sauce
1 teaspoon lemon pepper
3/4 cup cocktail sauce
1 pound lump crab meat, shells
    and cartilage removed and
    crab meat drained
2 cups (8 ounces) shredded
    Monterey Jack cheese
3 green onions, chopped
1/2 green bell pepper, chopped
1/2 cup sliced black olives

method

Beat the cream cheese in a mixing bowl at medium speed until smooth. Add the lemon juice, mayonnaise, Worcestershire sauce and lemon pepper and beat until blended. Spread the cream cheese mixture in a serving dish and chill, covered, for 20 minutes or longer.

Spread the cocktail sauce evenly over the cream cheese mixture. Top with the crab meat, Monterey Jack cheese, green onions, bell pepper and olives. Serve with assorted party crackers.

RED PESTO

Makes 1 1/2 cups

ingredients

1 cup boiling water
3 ounces sun-dried tomatoes
1 cup packed fresh parsley
3/4 cup extra-virgin olive oil
1/4 cup (1 ounce) grated
    Parmesan cheese
4 garlic cloves
2 baguettes, cut into 1-inch slices

method

Pour the boiling water over the sun-dried tomatoes in a heatproof bowl and let stand for 2 minutes. Drain and pat dry with paper towels.

Combine the sun-dried tomatoes, parsley, olive oil, cheese and garlic in a food processor and process until smooth. Serve with the baguette slices.

HOT BACON AND SWISS DIP

Serves 10 to 12

ingredients

8 ounces cream cheese, softened
1 cup mayonnaise
1 cup (4 ounces) shredded
    Swiss cheese
4 green onions, chopped
1/2 teaspoon Tabasco sauce
8 slices bacon, crisp-cooked
    and crumbled
1 cup butter cracker crumbs
Paprika to taste
Chopped fresh parsley to taste

method

Combine the cream cheese, mayonnaise, Swiss cheese, green onions and Tabasco sauce in a mixing bowl and beat until combined, scraping the bowl occasionally. Spread the cream cheese mixture in a 2 1/2-cup baking dish or a 9-inch round baking dish and sprinkle with the bacon and cracker crumbs.

Bake at 350 degrees for 15 to 20 minutes or until bubbly. Sprinkle lightly with paprika and parsley and serve with assorted party crackers.

WINTER FRUIT SALAD

Serves 10 to 12

ingredients

1 head lettuce, shredded
Sections of 4 oranges
4 unpeeled red apples, thinly sliced
4 bananas, sliced
1 pineapple, peeled and thinly sliced
3 kiwifruit, peeled and thinly sliced
1/4 cup sugar
1 cup chopped pecans
1 cup orange juice, tart French
    salad dressing or poppy seed
    salad dressing

method

Line a large salad bowl with the shredded lettuce and arrange the oranges, apples, bananas, pineapple and kiwifruit in the prepared bowl. Sprinkle with the sugar and pecans. Just before serving, drizzle with the orange juice and toss lightly.

PEPPER JELLY–GLAZED CARROTS

Serves 6

ingredients

2 pounds baby carrots
1 (10-ounce) can condensed
  chicken broth
2 tablespoons butter
1 (10-ounce) jar red pepper jelly

method

Bring the carrots and broth to a boil in a skillet over medium-high heat. Cook for 6 to 8 minutes or until the carrots are tender-crisp and the broth is reduced to $1/4$ cup, stirring frequently. Add the butter and jelly and cook for 5 minutes or until the mixture is thickened and the carrots are glazed, stirring constantly. Serve immediately.

AWESOME AU GRATIN POTATOES

Serves 8 to 10

ingredients

8 baking potatoes, peeled and thinly
  sliced (about 2 pounds)
2 cups (8 ounces) shredded
  Cheddar cheese
1 (10-ounce) can Cheddar
  cheese soup
$3/4$ cup milk
$1/8$ teaspoon pepper
2 garlic cloves, minced
$1/4$ cup (1 ounce) freshly grated
  Parmesan cheese
$1/4$ teaspoon paprika

method

Arrange the potatoes in a buttered baking dish. Combine the Cheddar cheese, soup, milk, pepper and garlic in a bowl and mix well. Pour the cheese mixture over the potatoes and sprinkle with the Parmesan cheese and paprika.

Bake, covered with foil, at 400 degrees for 1 hour. Remove the foil and bake for 15 to 20 minutes longer or until brown and bubbly.

TURNIP GREENS CASSEROLE

Serves 4 to 6

ingredients

2 large cans turnip greens, spinach
 or kale
1 (10-ounce) can cream of
 mushroom soup
1/2 cup mayonnaise
2 tablespoons vinegar
2 teaspoons prepared horseradish
2 eggs, beaten
1/2 teaspoon salt
1/2 teaspoon pepper
1/2 to 1 cup saltine cracker crumbs
1 cup (4 ounces) shredded sharp
 Cheddar cheese

method

Combine the turnip greens, soup, mayonnaise, vinegar, prepared horseradish, eggs, salt and pepper in a bowl and mix well. Spoon the turnip greens mixture into a 9×13-inch baking dish sprayed with nonstick cooking spray.

Bake at 350 degrees for 30 to 35 minutes. Sprinkle with the cracker crumbs and cheese and bake for 5 to 10 minutes longer or until the cheese melts. You may substitute 4 cups drained cooked fresh turnip greens for the canned turnip greens.

CREAMY WHITE CHICKEN CHILI

Serves 6 to 8

ingredients

1 tablespoon olive oil
4 to 6 boneless skinless chicken
 breasts, cut into bite-size pieces
1 onion, chopped
6 (15-ounce) cans white beans
2 (4-ounce) cans diced green chiles
2 teaspoons ground cumin
1 1/2 teaspoons oregano
1/2 teaspoon chili powder
1/2 teaspoon cayenne pepper
49 ounces chicken broth
2 cups sour cream

method

Heat the olive oil in a stockpot and add the chicken. Cook for several minutes and stir in the onion. Sauté until the onion is tender. Add the undrained beans, green chiles, cumin, oregano, chili powder and cayenne pepper and mix well. Stir in the broth and sour cream. Simmer for 2 to 3 hours or to the desired consistency, stirring occasionally. Ladle into chili bowls and serve with white corn chips and shredded Cheddar cheese.

REAL CAJUN RED BEANS AND RICE

Serves 6 to 8

ingredients

1 pound dried red beans
2 quarts water
8 ounces salt pork
Salt to taste
3 cups chopped onions
1 bunch green onions, chopped
1 cup fresh parsley, chopped
1 cup chopped bell pepper
1 (4-ounce) can tomato sauce
2 large garlic cloves, crushed
1 tablespoon salt
1 tablespoon Worcestershire sauce
1 teaspoon black pepper
1 teaspoon red pepper
1/4 teaspoon oregano
1/4 teaspoon thyme
3 dashes of Tabasco sauce
1 pound link sausage, sliced
Hot cooked rice

method

Sort and rinse the beans. Combine the beans with a generous amount of water in a bowl and soak for 8 to 10 hours; drain. Combine the beans, 2 quarts water, the salt pork and salt to taste in a large stockpot and bring to a boil. Reduce the heat and simmer for 45 minutes. Stir in the onions, green onions, parsley, bell pepper, tomato sauce and garlic. Add 1 tablespoon salt, the Worcestershire sauce, black pepper, red pepper, oregano, thyme and Tabasco sauce and mix well.

Simmer for 1 hour, stirring occasionally. Add the sausage and cook for 45 minutes. Remove from the heat and let stand until cool; do not chill. Return the bean mixture to the heat and bring to a boil. Reduce the heat to low and simmer for 30 to 40 minutes or to the desired consistency, stirring occasionally. Serve over hot cooked rice.

*F*or an easier foolproof alternative to cooking the beans on the stovetop, soak the beans for 8 to 10 hours. Drain the beans and combine with the remaining ingredients in a slow cooker. Cook, covered, on Low for about 8 hours. Ladle over hot cooked rice.

CAJUN STRATA

- -

Serves 8

ingredients

2 tablespoons butter
2 cups sliced fresh mushrooms
   (8 ounces)
1 cup chopped onion
1/2 cup chopped celery
2 garlic cloves, minced
8 cups cubed French bread
1 pound andouille,
   thinly sliced
12 ounces Cheddar cheese,
   shredded
1/2 cup chopped green onions
2 cups milk
4 eggs, lightly beaten
1 tablespoon Dijon mustard
1 teaspoon salt
1 teaspoon ground cumin
1/4 teaspoon black pepper
1/4 teaspoon cayenne pepper

method

Melt the butter in a skillet and add the mushrooms, onion, celery and garlic. Sauté for 5 minutes or until the vegetables are tender. Layer one-half of the bread cubes, one-half of the sausage, one-half of the cheese, one-half of the sautéed vegetables and all the green onions in a lightly oiled 9×13-inch baking dish. Top with the remaining bread cubes, the remaining sausage, the remaining cheese and the remaining sautéed vegetables.

Whisk the milk, eggs, Dijon mustard, salt, cumin, black pepper and cayenne pepper in a bowl until blended and pour the egg mixture over the prepared layers. Chill, covered, for 8 to 10 hours. Bake, uncovered, at 350 degrees for 1 hour.

*C*otton and lumber were the economic lifeblood of Northwest Louisiana during the nineteenth century. By the twentieth century, Northwest Louisiana was the center of the nation's oil industry, a title later lost to Houston, Texas.

SHRIMP ÉTOUFFÉE

Serves 4 to 6

ingredients

3/4 cup (1 1/2 sticks) butter
4 cups chopped onions
2 cups chopped bell peppers
2 cups chopped celery
2 teaspoons minced garlic
2 pounds medium shrimp, peeled
    and deveined
2 teaspoons salt
1/2 teaspoon cayenne pepper
2 tablespoons all-purpose flour
2 cups water
1/2 cup chopped green onions
6 tablespoons chopped
    fresh parsley
Hot cooked rice

method

Melt the butter in a large skillet over medium heat. Stir in the onions, bell peppers and celery. Sauté for 10 minutes or until the vegetables are tender and golden brown. Stir in the garlic and cook for 2 minutes. Add the shrimp, salt and cayenne pepper and cook for 4 minutes or until the shrimp turn pink, stirring frequently.

Dissolve the flour in the water in a small bowl and add to the shrimp mixture. Cook until slightly thickened, stirring frequently. Reduce the heat to medium-low and simmer for 6 to 8 minutes, stirring occasionally. Add the green onions and parsley and cook for 2 minutes longer, stirring occasionally. Serve over hot cooked rice.

JAMBALAYA

Serves 8 to 10

ingredients

3 to 4 pounds shrimp, cooked,
    peeled and deveined
1 pound andouille, sliced
1 cup chopped green onions
1 cup fresh parsley, finely chopped
3/4 cup chopped bell pepper
2 cups uncooked rice
4 bay leaves
1 (10-ounce) can French onion soup
1 (10-ounce) can beef broth
1 (8-ounce) can tomato sauce
1/2 cup water
1 teaspoon salt
1/2 teaspoon cayenne pepper
Black pepper to taste
1/2 cup (1 stick) butter or margarine,
    cut into pieces

method

Layer the shrimp, sausage, green onions, parsley and bell pepper in a deep baking dish. Top with the rice and bay leaves. Mix the soup, broth, tomato sauce, water, salt, cayenne pepper and black pepper in a bowl and pour over the prepared layers. Dot with the butter.

Bake, covered with foil, at 350 degrees for 1 1/2 hours. Discard the bay leaves and spoon the jambalaya into bowls. May prepare several days in advance and store, covered, in the refrigerator. Reheat before serving. Or, freeze for future use. May substitute 1 shredded cooked chicken or 2 shredded cooked ducks for the shrimp.

MARDI GRAS KING CAKE

This recipe has a lot of steps, but none of them are difficult. Now that you know how time-consuming it is to make a King Cake, you can appreciate why many people just order one from their favorite bakery!

Serves 15

ingredients

CAKE

- 1/2 cup warm water (110 to 115 degrees)
- 2 envelopes dry yeast
- 1/2 cup plus 1 teaspoon sugar
- 3 1/2 to 4 1/2 cups all-purpose flour
- 2 teaspoons salt
- 1 teaspoon ground nutmeg
- 1 teaspoon grated lemon zest
- 1/2 cup warm milk
- 5 egg yolks
- 1/2 cup (1 stick) plus 2 tablespoons butter, softened
- 1 teaspoon ground cinnamon
- 1 egg
- 1 tablespoon milk
- 1 (1-inch) plastic baby doll

method

CAKE

Pour the warm water into a small shallow bowl and sprinkle with the yeast and 2 teaspoons of the sugar. Let rest for 3 minutes and then stir to mix. Let stand in a warm place for 10 minutes or until the yeast bubbles.

Sift the remaining sugar, 3 1/2 cups of the flour, the salt and nutmeg into a large mixing bowl and stir in the lemon zest. Make a well in the center of the flour mixture and add the yeast mixture, warm milk and egg yolks to the well. Mix with a wooden spoon until smooth. Add 1/2 cup of the butter 1 tablespoon at a time, beating well after each addition. Continue beating for 2 minutes longer or until the dough can be shaped into a medium soft ball.

Place the dough on a lightly floured surface and knead until the dough is no longer sticky, gradually adding up to 1 cup of the remaining flour. Knead for 10 minutes longer or until shiny and elastic. Coat a large bowl with 1 tablespoon of the remaining butter and place the dough in the prepared bowl, turning to coat the surface. Let rise, covered with a heavy kitchen towel, in a warm place for 1 1/2 hours or until doubled in bulk. Remove the dough to a floured surface and punch the dough down. Sprinkle with the cinnamon and then pat and shape the dough into a long snake or cylinder. Form a twist by folding the long cylinder in half, end to end, and pinching the ends together. Twist the dough and shape into a ring, pinching the ends together.

ingredients

POURED ICING

3/4 cup confectioners' sugar

1/4 cup lemon juice

2 1/4 cups water

Purple-, yellow- and green-tinted
  sugars

Place the ring on a baking sheet coated with the remaining 1 tablespoon butter. Let rise, covered with a kitchen towel, for 45 minutes or until doubled in bulk.

Brush the top and side of the cake with a mixture of the egg and 1 tablespoon milk. Bake at 375 degrees for 25 to 35 minutes or until golden brown. Cool on a wire rack and hide the plastic baby doll in the cake.

ICING

Combine the confectioners' sugar, lemon juice and water in a bowl and mix until of a spreading consistency, adding additional water if needed for the desired consistency. Drizzle the icing over the cake and immediately sprinkle with the tinted sugars, alternating among the three colors. Let stand until set and cut into 2- to 3-inch pieces.

The King Cake is a traditional Mardi Gras treat, baked and covered with a poured sugar topping in Mardi Gras colors: purple, representing Justice; green, representing Faith; and gold, representing Power. Traditionally, the person who finds the hidden "baby" in his or her slice of cake must provide the cake the next year. Hundreds of thousands of King Cakes are consumed at parties worldwide every year and in fact, a Mardi Gras party would not be complete without one.

EASY KING CAKE

Serves 16

ingredients

2 (8-count) cans refrigerator
  cinnamon rolls
Yellow, green and purple sprinkles
1 plastic baby doll
1/4 cup confectioners' sugar
  (optional)
1 tablespoon milk (optional)

method

Arrange the cinnamon rolls in a circle with sides touching on a baking sheet. Bake using the package directions. Immediately spread with the icing that accompanied the cinnamon rolls and sprinkle with the colored sprinkles. Push the plastic baby doll into the cake from the bottom so that it is not visible from the top. If additional icing is required, spread with a mixture of the confectioners' sugar and milk.

OREO BALLS

Makes 3 dozen

ingredients

8 ounces cream cheese, softened
1 package Oreos, finely crushed
1 cup (6 ounces) semisweet
  chocolate chips
1 1/2 cups (9 ounces) white
  chocolate chips

method

Combine the cream cheese and cookie crumbs in a bowl and mix well. (Chill if needed to shape the mixture.) Shape the cookie mixture into balls and arrange on a baking sheet lined with waxed paper. Chill for 1 hour.

Pour the semisweet chocolate chips into a microwave-safe bowl and microwave until melted. Roll the chilled balls in the chocolate and return to the baking sheet. Chill until set. Microwave the white chocolate chips in a microwave-safe bowl until melted and pour into a sealable plastic bag. Seal tightly and snip one corner of the bag. Drizzle the white chocolate over the chilled balls and chill until set.

WHITE CHOCOLATE MACADAMIA CRÈME BRÛLÉE

This recipe comes from Chef David Bridges of Bella Fresca.

Serves 8

ingredients

8 ounces white chocolate

1 quart heavy cream

8 egg yolks, lightly beaten

4 ounces macadamia nuts, chopped

1/2 cup turbinado sugar

method

Place the white chocolate in a stainless steel bowl. Bring the heavy cream to a simmer in a saucepan and pour over the chocolate, mixing until smooth. Stir a small amount of the hot chocolate mixture into the egg yolks; then stir the egg yolk mixture into the hot chocolate mixture.

Spoon the chocolate mixture into eight 6-ounce soufflé cups. Top each with 1 tablespoon of the macadamia nuts. Place the soufflé cups in a baking pan and add enough hot water to reach halfway up the sides of the cups.

Bake at 325 degrees for 40 minutes or until set. Remove to a wire rack and cool for 15 minutes. Sprinkle 1 tablespoon of the turbinado sugar over the top of each baked custard and caramelize using a culinary blowtorch. Serve immediately.

The Caddo Parish Mental Society and the Junior League cooperated on a survey to evaluate the community's health needs. Based on their findings, the League sponsored a child guidance center with a part-time staff for one year. In its second year, the center acquired a full-time caseworker and psychiatric services one day per week. The new Guidance Center was accepted by the Community Chest in 1952.

FOUR-LAYER LEMON DELIGHT

Serves 15

ingredients

2 cups all-purpose flour
1 cup (2 sticks) butter, melted
1 cup finely chopped pecans
8 ounces cream cheese, softened
2 cups whipped topping
1 cup confectioners' sugar
1 (14-ounce) can sweetened
   condensed milk
3 egg yolks
1/3 cup fresh lemon juice
1 1/2 to 2 cups whipped topping

method

Combine the flour, butter and pecans in a bowl and mix well. Press the pecan mixture over the bottom of a 9×13-inch baking pan and bake at 350 degrees for 20 minutes or until light brown. Let stand until cool.

Combine the cream cheese, 2 cups whipped topping and the confectioners' sugar in a mixing bowl and beat until smooth. Spread the cream cheese mixture over the baked layer. Whisk the condensed milk, egg yolks and lemon juice in a bowl until blended and pour over the prepared layers. Spread with 1 1/2 to 2 cups whipped topping. Chill, covered, until serving time.

If you are concerned about using raw egg yolks, use yolks from eggs pasteurized in their shells, which are sold at some specialty food stores, or use an equivalent amount of pasteurized egg substitute.

In the spring of 1968, the Caddo Parish School Board approved the recommendation of the Junior League and the Council of Jewish Women to initiate two programs for children with learning disabilities. The first was designed to help children experiencing difficulty in school by getting them one-on-one help three days a week. The second program, called Developmental First Grade, was designed to identify, through testing of kindergarten children, those who might experience academic difficulties in their school years ahead. The School Board assumed the responsibility of administering this program in 1972.

MARCH

As the days grow longer and warmer, the landscape

of Northwest Louisiana erupts into a beautiful

jonquil jubilee

display of floral color. Nature paints a beautiful

blooming on the bricks

backdrop for several March festivals celebrating

redbud festival

the transformation of spring.

easter

Days get longer and warmer quickly in Northwest Louisiana as spring approaches. In one of the most colorful months of the year, the region's flowers come alive and burst into full bloom, and that's reason enough for us to celebrate. In March, after the Mardi Gras memories fade, the fun continues with several festivals and parades, most of which are in celebration of the flowers of the region.

On the first Saturday of March, the JONQUIL JUBILEE in Gibsland is held in honor of the daffodil. There you will discover a wide variety of historic tours, antiques, artists, live music, and delicious food, including "famous" teacakes and the Lion's Club pancake breakfast. You can also visit the Bonnie and Clyde Ambush Museum, which occupies the historical location of Ma Canfield's Café where Bonnie and Clyde dined for the last time.

Experience something you can't find in history books and watch Louisiana's colorful past come to life at the Sacred Places Tour in the heart of the Historic Landmark District in Natchitoches. This guided tour, complete with character portrayals, explores the history of the oldest-known cemetery in the Louisiana Purchase, dating back to 1797.

The LOUISIANA REDBUD FESTIVAL is held on the third Saturday in March in Vivian. This festival celebrates one of our most beautiful native flowering trees with arts, crafts, a carnival, parade, and the Miss Redbud Pageant. The flowers of this magnificently adorned tree are said to have an agreeable acidic taste and are frequently used in salads and for making pickle relish, while the inner bark has been used to make a mustard-yellow textile dye.

Natchitoches residents celebrate the arrival of spring at the BLOOMING ON THE BRICKS FESTIVAL in historic downtown along the banks of the scenic Cane River Lake. Gardening seminars, demonstrations, vendors, entertainment, and children's activities are all included at this Natchitoches Main Street event. You can bet that good food will be abundant, too.

As nature begins its annual rebirth, March is also a month for spiritual rebirth, as many Christians in Northwest Louisiana prepare for EASTER. This religious holiday celebrates the resurrection of Christ and marks the end of Lent. It may occur on any Sunday between March 22nd and April 25th, and though the algorithm to calculate the true day of Easter is anything but simple, it is celebrated on the first Sunday after the first full moon after the spring equinox. On this day you will find children carefully dressed in their finest new clothes as families gather at teas and brunches to celebrate the holiday amidst the flowers and flavors of spring.

March is a gorgeous time of year in Northwest Louisiana, and as you can see, we take full advantage of the opportunity to celebrate nature's seasonal transformation.

BEST TEA PUNCH*

Makes 1 gallon

2 cups water
2 cups sugar
8 tea bags, or 2 family-size tea bags
2 cups orange juice
2/3 cup lemon juice
2 quarts cold water
Sprigs of mint

*Photograph for this recipe on page 45.

Combine 2 cups water and the sugar in a saucepan and bring to a boil. Boil for 5 minutes. Remove from the heat and add the tea bags to the sugar syrup. Steep for 5 to 10 minutes.

Pour the tea mixture into a 1-gallon pitcher and squeeze the tea bags to remove any remaining tea. Discard the tea bags. Add the orange juice, lemon juice and 2 quarts cold water and mix well. Add enough ice to fill the pitcher. Pour into glasses and garnish each serving with a sprig of mint.

OPEN-FACE CUCUMBER SANDWICHES*

Makes 45 sandwiches

8 ounces cream cheese, softened
1/2 envelope Italian salad
    dressing mix
1 cucumber, peeled and thinly sliced
1 loaf cocktail hearty rye bread
Chopped fresh dill weed

*Photograph for this recipe on page 45.

Beat the cream cheese and salad dressing mix in a bowl until blended. Spread the cream cheese mixture on one side of each bread slice and top each with 1 cucumber slice. Sprinkle with dill weed and serve immediately.

PARTY SANDWICHES*

Makes 2 dozen sandwiches

ingredients

1 (24-count) package party rolls
1/2 cup (1 stick) butter
1/4 cup prepared mustard
1 to 2 tablespoons poppy seeds
1 tablespoon dried minced onion
8 ounces sliced ham
8 ounces thinly sliced Swiss cheese

*Photograph for this recipe on page 45.

method

Split the rolls horizontally into two layers; do not separate into individual rolls. Melt the butter in a saucepan and stir in the prepared mustard, poppy seeds and onion. Spread the cut sides of the rolls with the butter mixture.

Layer the sliced ham and sliced cheese over the bottom roll layer, adding additional layers as desired. Top with the remaining roll layer. Wrap the stuffed rolls in foil and place on a baking sheet. Bake at 350 degrees for 15 minutes.

CARROT NUT SANDWICH FILLING*

A great crunchy alternative to cucumber sandwiches. You may freeze the sandwiches for future use, if desired.
Makes 2 to 3 cups

ingredients

8 ounces cream cheese, softened
1/2 cup (or more) mayonnaise
1 cup ground pecans
1 cup grated carrots
1 teaspoon garlic powder, or to taste
1/2 teaspoon sugar
1/4 teaspoon salt

*Photograph for this recipe on page 45.

method

Beat the cream cheese and mayonnaise in a bowl until creamy. Stir in the pecans, carrots, garlic powder, sugar and salt. Spread on party bread and/or assorted party crackers.

CHIANTI'S EGGPLANT ROLLS IN TOMATO SAUCE

. . . .

This signature dish is from Chianti Restaurant's Executive Chef, Enrico Giacalone.
Serves 2

ingredients

SIMPLE TOMATO SAUCE

1 (14-ounce) can peeled
    whole tomatoes
2 tablespoons extra-virgin olive oil
1 tablespoon chopped garlic
2 tablespoons chopped fresh basil
1 teaspoon sugar
Salt and pepper to taste

EGGPLANT ROLLS AND
ASSEMBLY

4 (1/4-inch) lengthwise
    slices eggplant
Salt to taste
3 tablespoons extra-virgin olive oil
1 tablespoon chopped garlic
1 tablespoon chopped fresh
    flat-leaf parsley
Pepper to taste
6 ounces ricotta cheese
2 ounces mozzarella cheese,
    shredded
1 ounce Parmesan cheese, grated or
    shredded
1 ounce pecorino cheese, grated
    (optional for sharpness)
1 tablespoon chopped fresh
    flat-leaf parsley
Grated pecorino cheese to taste

method

SAUCE

Crush the tomatoes in a bowl using a fork. Heat the olive oil in a 2-quart saucepan over medium heat and add the garlic. Cook until the garlic is tender but not brown, stirring frequently. Stir in the crushed tomatoes, basil, sugar, salt and pepper. Bring to a boil and reduce the heat to low. Simmer for 10 minutes, stirring occasionally. Process the tomato sauce in a blender until puréed and return to the saucepan. Keep warm over low heat.

ROLLS

Sprinkle the eggplant slices with salt and place in a colander to purge the bitterness. Let stand for 20 minutes. Whisk the olive oil, garlic, 1 tablespoon parsley, salt and pepper in a bowl until combined.

Pat the eggplant slices dry with paper towels and brush both sides with the olive oil mixture. Grill the slices over hot coals until tender. Arrange on a greased baking sheet. Mix the ricotta cheese, mozzarella cheese, Parmesan cheese, 1 ounce pecorino cheese, salt and pepper in a bowl and spread one-fourth of the cheese mixture on each slice. Roll to enclose the filling and arrange the rolls on the same baking sheet. Bake, covered with foil, at 350 degrees for 10 minutes.

Ladle about 1/2 cup of the tomato sauce onto each of two serving plates, using just enough of the tomato sauce to line the bottoms of the plates. Arrange two rolls on each prepared plate and sprinkle with 1 tablespoon parsley and pecorino cheese to taste. Serve immediately.

STRAWBERRY ORANGE SALAD WITH CITRUS DRESSING*

Serves 6 to 8

ingredients

SUGARED PECANS
2/3 cup pecan halves
1/4 cup sugar

CITRUS DRESSING AND SALAD
3 navel oranges
2/3 cup canola oil
1/4 cup fresh lime juice (3 to 4 limes)
2 tablespoons sugar
1 teaspoon grated lime zest
1 teaspoon grated orange zest
1 package spring mix salad greens
1 quart fresh strawberries,
   quartered

*Photograph for this recipe on page 45.

method

PECANS

Cook the pecans and sugar in a skillet over low heat until the sugar dissolves and the pecans are coated, stirring frequently. Spread on a sheet of foil and let stand until cool. Break into pieces.

DRESSING AND SALAD

Section the oranges over a bowl, reserving 2 tablespoons of the orange juice. Whisk the reserved juice, canola oil, lime juice, sugar, lime zest and orange zest in a bowl until combined. Gently toss the salad greens, oranges and strawberries in a bowl. Add the dressing and pecans and mix well. Serve immediately.

CHICKEN MANGO SALAD

Serves 6

ingredients

1 cup sour cream
1/2 cup mango chutney or other
   flavor chutney, such as Major Grey's
1/4 cup mayonnaise
1 tablespoon honey
1 1/2 teaspoons grated fresh ginger
1 teaspoon curry powder
1/2 teaspoon salt
12 ounces rotelle or fusilli
2 cups shredded cooked chicken
1 mango, peeled and
   coarsely chopped
2/3 cup thinly sliced celery
1 cup red seedless grapes,
   cut into halves
3/4 cup slivered almonds, toasted
1/4 cup chopped green bell pepper
Whole grapes

method

Combine the sour cream, chutney, mayonnaise, honey, ginger, curry powder and salt in a bowl and mix well. Let stand at room temperature.

Cook the pasta using the package directions until al dente and drain. Rinse with cold water and drain again. Mix the pasta, chicken and 1 cup of the dressing in a bowl until coated. Add the mango, celery, grape halves, 1/2 cup of the almonds and the bell pepper to the chicken mixture and chill, covered, in the refrigerator. Chill the remaining dressing. Remove the salad 30 minutes before serving and stir in the remaining dressing. Taste and adjust the seasonings. Sprinkle with the remaining 1/4 cup almonds and garnish with whole grapes.

ASPARAGUS WITH WHITE WINE VINAIGRETTE

Serves 6 to 8

ingredients

WHITE WINE VINAIGRETTE

1/2 teaspoon salt
1/2 teaspoon sugar
1/2 teaspoon dry mustard
1/3 teaspoon paprika
2/3 cup extra-virgin olive oil
1/3 cup white wine vinegar
2 to 4 tablespoons Tabasco sauce
1 garlic clove, crushed

SALAD

2 pounds asparagus spears
2 or 3 tomatoes, sliced
8 pitted black olives
8 mushrooms, sliced

method

VINAIGRETTE

Combine the salt, sugar, dry mustard and paprika in a bowl and mix well. Add the olive oil, vinegar, Tabasco sauce and garlic and whisk until combined. Pour into a shallow dish.

SALAD

Snap off and discard the thick woody ends of the asparagus spears. Steam the asparagus until tender-crisp. Immediately plunge the asparagus into a bowl of ice water to stop the cooking process and drain. Add the asparagus, tomatoes, olives and mushrooms to the vinaigrette and turn to coat. Let stand at room temperature for 1 hour, turning occasionally. Drain the vegetables and arrange on a platter.

If using asparagus in a chilled dish, plunge the asparagus into cold water immediately after cooking to stop the cooking process and preserve the bright green color.

KNOCCHI

Serves 8

ingredients

1 quart milk
1/2 cup (1 stick) butter
1 cup grits (do not use instant)
1 cup (4 ounces) grated
   Gruyère cheese
1 cup (4 ounces) shredded
   Cheddar cheese
1 teaspoon salt
1/8 teaspoon pepper
1/3 cup butter, melted

method

Bring the milk to a boil in a saucepan and stir in 1/2 cup butter. Add the grits gradually, whisking constantly. Bring to a boil and cook for 5 minutes or until thickened, stirring constantly. Remove from the heat and beat with an electric mixer for 5 minutes or until creamy. Spread in a 9×13-inch baking dish and chill for 2 to 10 hours. Cut into rectangular pieces and remove to a platter. Arrange like fallen dominoes in the same baking dish. Sprinkle with the cheese, salt and pepper and drizzle with 1/3 cup butter. Bake at 400 degrees for 30 minutes.

CAJUN CATFISH WITH STRAWBERRY SAUCE

Serves 6

ingredients

CATFISH
2 to 2 1/2 pounds catfish fillets
Salt and pepper to taste
Hot pepper sauce to taste
3/4 cup cornmeal
3/4 cup all-purpose flour
1 cup vegetable oil for frying

STRAWBERRY SAUCE
   AND ASSEMBLY
1 (12-ounce) jar strawberry
   preserves
1 tablespoon soy sauce
1/2 cup strawberry vinegar or red
   wine vinegar
1/4 cup cocktail sauce
2 tablespoons prepared horseradish
1 teaspoon minced garlic

method

CATFISH
Arrange the fillets in a shallow dish and sprinkle with salt and pepper and drizzle with hot pepper sauce. Chill, covered, for 1 hour and drain. Mix the cornmeal and flour in a shallow dish and coat the fillets in the cornmeal mixture. Heat the oil in a heavy skillet over medium-high heat and add the fillets. Fry until brown on both sides; drain. Keep warm in a 200-degree oven.

SAUCE
Mix the preserves, soy sauce, vinegar, cocktail sauce, prepared horseradish and garlic in a saucepan. Simmer over low heat to the desired consistency, stirring occasionally. Spoon 1/4 cup of the sauce onto each of six plates and top with the fillets. Garnish with fresh strawberries and sprigs of parsley. Serve immediately.

PASTA SAUCE RAPHAEL

Makes 8 pints

ingredients

2 (28-ounce) cans whole
   tomatoes, drained
1 (28-ounce) can whole tomatoes
1/4 cup olive oil
2 cups coarsely chopped
   yellow onions
1/2 cup finely chopped fresh parsley
1/4 cup chopped fresh basil
4 garlic cloves, minced
1 tablespoon dried oregano
1/4 teaspoon dried red pepper flakes
1 (28-ounce) can crushed tomatoes
1 teaspoon salt
1/2 teaspoon black pepper
3 (14-ounce) cans artichoke hearts,
   drained and cut into quarters
2 (16-ounce) cans tomato purée
1 tablespoon sugar
1/4 cup (1 ounce) grated Romano
   cheese

method

Process 2 drained cans of whole tomatoes and 1 undrained can of whole tomatoes in a food processor until coarsely chopped, or cut the tomatoes into quarters. Heat the olive oil in a Dutch oven over medium heat and add the onions, parsley, basil, garlic, oregano and red pepper flakes. Sauté for 5 minutes and stir in the processed tomatoes, undrained crushed tomatoes, salt and black pepper.

Simmer over medium heat for 1 hour, stirring occasionally. Add the artichokes and tomato purée and simmer for 1 hour longer, stirring frequently. Stir in the sugar and simmer until thickened, stirring occasionally. Stir in the cheese. Taste and adjust the seasonings. Serve over your favorite hot cooked pasta. This recipe makes enough sauce for four pounds of pasta. Freeze for future use, if desired.

*W*hen sautéing onions and garlic together, be sure to sauté the onions for at least one-half of the cooking time before adding the garlic. If the garlic is added to the skillet at the same time, it could possibly overcook and burn. When this happens, a chemical reaction occurs that can make the dish bitter.

Serves 8 to 10

ingredients

CHEESE GRITS
1/2 cup grits
1 cup (4 ounces) shredded Pepper
    Jack cheese
1/2 cup Cheez Whiz
2 tablespoons butter, softened
1/4 teaspoon Worcestershire sauce
1/4 teaspoon white pepper

SHRIMP
3 tablespoons butter
1 1/4 cups sliced fresh mushrooms
1 small onion, chopped
1 (14-ounce) can artichoke hearts,
    drained and quartered
2 tablespoons white wine
2 pounds fresh shrimp, cooked,
    peeled and deveined

WHITE SAUCE AND ASSEMBLY
3 tablespoons butter
3 tablespoons all-purpose flour
2 cups milk
1 teaspoon hot sauce
1/2 teaspoon salt
1/2 cup fine bread crumbs
1/4 cup (1 ounce) grated
    Parmesan cheese
1/2 cup (1 stick) butter, melted

method

GRITS
Cook the grits using the package directions. Combine the cooked grits, Pepper Jack cheese, Cheez Whiz, butter, Worcestershire sauce and white pepper in a bowl and mix well.

SHRIMP
Melt the butter in a skillet and add the mushrooms and onion. Sauté until tender and stir in the artichokes. Cook until heated through and stir in the wine. Cook until the wine evaporates, stirring occasionally. Combine the grits, artichoke mixture and shrimp in a bowl and mix well. Spread the shrimp mixture in a buttered 9×13-inch baking dish.

SAUCE
Melt 3 tablespoons butter in a saucepan and add the flour. Cook until bubbly, stirring constantly. Stir in the milk and bring to a boil. Cook until thickened, stirring constantly. Blend in the hot sauce and salt and spread the sauce over the shrimp mixture. Toss the bread crumbs and cheese in a bowl and sprinkle over the top. Drizzle with 1/2 cup melted butter. Bake at 350 degrees for 20 minutes or until brown and bubbly. You may prepare up to 1 day in advance and store, covered, in the refrigerator. Let stand at room temperature for 1 hour before baking.

BLACK BEAN WRAPS WITH PICO DE GALLO

Makes 10 to 12 wraps

PICO DE GALLO
3 plum tomatoes or Roma
   tomatoes, chopped
1/2 onion, chopped
Juice of 1 small lime
1/2 to 1 jalapeño chile, seeded
   and minced
1/4 teaspoon salt, or to taste
1 tablespoon minced fresh cilantro

BLACK BEAN WRAPS
8 ounces cream cheese, softened
1 cup (4 ounces) shredded Monterey
   Jack cheese
1/4 cup sour cream
1 to 3 tablespoons milk
1/2 teaspoon garlic salt
1 (15-ounce) can black beans,
   drained and rinsed
1/2 cup salsa
10 to 12 flour tortillas or whole wheat
   flour tortillas
10 ounces fresh spinach, trimmed
1 (7-ounce) jar roasted red bell
   peppers, drained and
   cut into strips
2 cups coarsely shredded carrots

PICO DE GALLO
Mix the tomatoes, onion, lime juice, jalapeño chile, salt and cilantro in a bowl. Chill, covered, in the refrigerator.

WRAPS
Beat the cream cheese, Monterey Jack cheese, sour cream, milk and garlic salt in a mixing bowl at medium speed until blended. Mash the beans and salsa in a bowl until combined using a potato masher.

Spread the cream cheese mixture over one side of each of the tortillas. Top evenly with the bean mixture and layer with the spinach, roasted peppers and carrots. Roll to enclose the filling and slice each wrap diagonally into halves. Serve with the pico de gallo.

*F*amous DJ and radio show host Wolfman Jack started his career broadcasting in Shreveport, and Mary Miles Minter, a famous silent movie actress, was born in Shreveport and spent her childhood in the Shreveport and Mansfield areas of Northwest Louisiana.

LEMON PULL-APARTS

Makes 2 dozen

ingredients

12 frozen yeast rolls, thawed but
   still cold
1/4 cup (1/2 stick) butter, melted
1/2 cup granulated sugar
Grated zest of 2 lemons
1 cup confectioners' sugar
2 tablespoons fresh lemon juice
1 tablespoon butter, melted

method

Cut the cold rolls into halves and arrange in a 12-inch deep-dish pizza pan or in a 9×13-inch baking dish sprayed with nonstick cooking spray. Drizzle with 1/4 cup butter. Mix the granulated sugar and lemon zest in a bowl and sprinkle one-half over the rolls. Cover with a sheet of plastic wrap sprayed with nonstick cooking spray and let rise until doubled in bulk.

Remove the plastic wrap and sprinkle with the remaining sugar mixture. Bake at 350 degrees for 20 to 25 minutes. Immediately remove the rolls to a wire rack. Mix the confectioners' sugar, lemon juice and 1 tablespoon butter in a bowl and drizzle over the hot pull-aparts.

STUFFED STRAWBERRIES*

Makes 2 dozen

ingredients

1/4 cup sliced almonds
24 fresh strawberries
8 ounces cream cheese, softened
1/4 to 1/2 cup confectioners' sugar
1 tablespoon vanilla extract
Grated chocolate

*Photograph for this recipe on page 45.

method

Spread the almonds in a single layer on a baking sheet and toast at 350 degrees for 10 minutes, stirring occasionally. Slice off the bottom tips of the strawberries and hollow out the centers.

Beat the cream cheese, confectioners' sugar and vanilla in a mixing bowl until light and fluffy. Spoon the cream cheese mixture into a decorator tube fitted with a star tip and pipe into the strawberries. Arrange the strawberries on a serving platter and top each with an almond slice. Sprinkle with the grated chocolate.

Serves 12

ingredients

CAKE

1 (16-ounce) package angel food
   cake mix
Confectioners' sugar

LEMON CREAM AND
   ASSEMBLY

8 ounces cream cheese, softened
1/2 cup confectioners' sugar
1 tablespoon lemon juice
2 teaspoons grated lemon zest
6 cups whole stemmed strawberries
   (2 pounds)
Granulated sugar to taste
Confectioners' sugar to taste

method

CAKE

Line a 10×15-inch jelly roll pan with waxed paper. Prepare the cake mix using the package directions and spread the batter in the prepared pan. Bake at 350 degrees for 20 to 24 minutes or until the top is light brown and springs back when lightly touched. Loosen the edges of the warm cake and invert onto a large wire rack. Discard the waxed paper and invert the cake onto a kitchen towel sprinkled lightly with confectioners' sugar. Roll the cake in the towel as for a jelly roll from the short side. Place on a wire rack to cool.

CREAM

Beat the cream cheese, confectioners' sugar, lemon juice and lemon zest in a mixing bowl until creamy, scraping the bowl occasionally. Unroll the cake and trim any hard edges. Spread the lemon cream to within 1/2 inch of the edges. Slice 1 cup of the strawberries and arrange in a single layer over the lemon cream. Roll to enclose the filling and arrange seam side down on a serving platter. Chill, covered, for 30 minutes or until the filling is firm.

Process 2 cups of the remaining strawberries in a blender until puréed. Taste and sweeten with granulated sugar, if desired. Cut the remaining 3 cups strawberries into quarters and sweeten with granulated sugar, if desired.

To serve, sprinkle the top of the cake roll with confectioners' sugar and cut into 12 equal slices. Arrange each slice on a dessert plate along with 1/4 cup of the quartered strawberries. Drizzle with 1 tablespoon of the puréed strawberries and serve immediately.

STRABERRY CAKE*

Serves 12

ingredients

CAKE
2³/₄ cups sifted cake flour
2¹/₂ teaspoons baking powder
1 cup (2 sticks) unsalted
   butter, softened
2 cups sugar
1 (3-ounce) package
   strawberry gelatin
4 eggs, at room temperature
1 cup milk, at room temperature
¹/₂ cup strawberry purée
1 tablespoon vanilla extract

STRAWBERRY CREAM
CHEESE FROSTING
³/₄ cup (1¹/₂ sticks) unsalted
   butter, softened
12 ounces cream cheese, softened
4¹/₂ to 5 cups confectioners'
   sugar, sifted
2 tablespoons strawberry purée

*Photograph for this recipe on page 45.

method

CAKE
Mix the cake flour and baking powder together. Beat the butter, sugar and gelatin in a mixing bowl until light and fluffy, scraping the side of the bowl occasionally. Add the eggs one at a time, beating well after each addition. Add the cake flour mixture alternately with the milk, mixing well after each addition and beginning and ending with the flour mixture. Stir in the purée and vanilla. Spread the batter evenly in three greased and floured 9-inch cake pans. Bake at 350 degrees for 25 to 30 minutes or until a wooden pick inserted in the centers of the layers comes out clean. Cool in the pans for 10 minutes and remove to a wire rack to cool completely.

FROSTING
Beat the butter and cream cheese in a mixing bowl until smooth. Add the confectioners' sugar gradually, beating constantly until of a spreading consistency. Stir in the purée until blended. Spread the frosting between the layers and over the top and side of the cake.

NOTE: *Process frozen sweetened strawberries in a blender or food processor for the strawberry purée.*

*O*ur affiliation with Dress for Success, a national nonprofit organization that helps low-income women make the transition from welfare to the workforce, began in 1999. League members help these women find appropriate clothing in which to interview and then provide another suit once they find employment.

BLACK FOREST BROWNIES*

Makes 1⅓ to 2 dozen brownies

ingredients

BROWNIES

¾ cup plus 2 tablespoons
  all-purpose flour
¼ teaspoon baking powder
¼ teaspoon baking soda
⅛ teaspoon salt
1 cup sugar
⅔ cup baking cocoa
¼ cup (½ stick) butter, melted
1 egg
2 tablespoons water
1 teaspoon vanilla extract
¼ cup chopped candied cherries
3 tablespoons coarsely
  chopped walnuts

ALMOND GLAZE

½ cup sifted confectioners' sugar
1¾ teaspoons hot water
¼ teaspoon almond extract

*Photograph for this recipe on page 45.

method

BROWNIES

Coat the bottom of an 8×8-inch baking pan with nonstick cooking spray; do not coat the sides. Combine the flour, baking powder, baking soda and salt in a bowl and mix well. Whisk the sugar, baking cocoa, butter, egg, water and vanilla in a bowl until blended. Add the sugar mixture to the flour mixture and stir just until moistened. Stir in the cherries and walnuts and spread the batter in the prepared baking pan.

Bake at 350 degrees for 35 minutes or until a wooden pick inserted in the center comes out almost clean. Cool in the pan on a wire rack. You may substitute chopped plumped dried cherries for the candied cherries.

GLAZE

Combine the confectioners' sugar, hot water and flavoring in a bowl and mix well. Drizzle over the cooled brownies. Let stand for 15 minutes before cutting.

In 1945, Junior League members began cataloguing, processing, and performing other work for the city's only circulating library. South Highlands Elementary School took over this service in 1953.

APRIL

The chill of winter is all but a memory as the

activity heats up to keep pace with the weather.

first bloom celebration

Northwest Louisiana's flowers are at the peak

holiday in dixie

of their splendor in April, and it's a lovely time

artbreak

of year to gather with family and friends.

barksdale air force base
open house and air show

With April's arrival the weather has warmed, and we begin to settle comfortably into spring. You will find Northwest Louisiana engulfed in a kaleidoscope of colorful azaleas, including white, purple, pink, red, orange, and yellow. See them in full bloom at the Norton Art Gallery in Shreveport, where many photographers find nature's colorful backdrop among the beautiful flowers ideal for family and bridal portraits.

You can't talk of flowers without mentioning America's national flower, and Northwest Louisiana proudly claims America's largest garden dedicated to the rose. This magnificent flower is celebrated with the FIRST BLOOM CELEBRATION every April at The American Rose Center, which is located just a few minutes west of Shreveport. With sixty separate gardens displaying 20,000 magnificent roses, this 118-acre park is a must-see springtime showcase.

If you have kids, Shreveport is a great place to be in April. HOLIDAY IN DIXIE, an event steeped in tradition, has been honored by the Southeast Tourism Society as one of the Top 20 events for the month of April. This ten-day festival began in 1949 to celebrate the arrival of spring and the signing of the Louisiana Purchase. It continues today with more than fifty events including a carnival, the Miss Holiday in Dixie Pageant, block parties, a treasure hunt, and a parade complete with B-52 and A-10 flyovers courtesy of Barksdale Air Force Base.

In late April to early May, look to the sky for the annual BARKSDALE AIR FORCE BASE DEFENDERS OF LIBERTY OPEN HOUSE AND AIR SHOW. In addition to the spectacular displays of flying skill and precision, you'll find enough activities to fill an entire weekend. The kids will love the "Adventures in Aviation" kid's area, featuring aviation-themed activities including moonwalks, rock climbing, pedal airplane rides, and an interactive children's art display.

The Shreveport Regional Arts Council hosts ARTBREAK, Louisiana's largest arts festival for kids, during the month of April. This six-day children's favorite is a hands-on arts festival showcasing and celebrating the visual arts, literature, music, theatre, and performing arts in Caddo Parish Schools.

April is also the time of the year for the area's annual "society" events. Almost no expense is spared at the Cotillion Club Ball, an elaborate black-tie dinner and dance honoring community leaders and their families. And at the Plantation Ball, a formal-attire presentation of the sons and daughters of area planters, locals help keep the Southern plantation heritage of the area alive.

As you can see, Northwest Louisiana gets creative about its reasons to celebrate, and in April celebrations abound.

PEACH PARTY PUNCH

Serves 20

ingredients

1 (2-liter) bottle peach soda

1 (12-ounce) can frozen orange
juice concentrate, thawed

1 (750-milliliter) bottle sparkling
white grape juice

1 (750-milliliter) bottle Champagne
(optional)

method

Combine the soda, orange juice concentrate, grape juice and Champagne in a large container and mix well. Serve over ice in glasses.

TOMATO CUPS

Makes 20

ingredients

1 (10-count) can country biscuits

2/3 cup mayonnaise

2 cups (8 ounces) shredded
mozzarella cheese

1/4 cup (1 ounce) grated
Parmesan cheese

2 tablespoons snipped fresh basil,
or 2 teaspoons dried basil

1 garlic clove, crushed

Salt to taste

7 cherry tomatoes, each
cut into 3 slices

method

Cut the biscuits into halves. Roll each half into a ball and roll the balls into rounds on a lightly floured surface. Press each round over the bottom and up the side of a miniature muffin cup.

Mix the mayonnaise, mozzarella cheese, Parmesan cheese, basil and garlic in a bowl and season with salt. Arrange 1 tomato slice in the bottom of each prepared muffin cup and spoon some of the mayonnaise mixture over the tomatoes. Bake at 375 degrees for 15 to 20 minutes or until golden brown and bubbly. Serve warm. You may have some of the filling left over.

CHEEZIES

* *

These are a hit with everyone from children to grandparents. Serve these
at parties or showers, for breakfast, or as a snack.

Serves 10

ingredients

2 (5-ounce) jars Old English
   cheese spread
3/4 cup (1 1/2 sticks) butter, softened
1 egg
1 loaf white bread

method

Beat the cheese spread, butter and egg in a mixing bowl until creamy. Stack 2 slices of the bread and trim the crusts. Spread the cheese mixture on one side of one of the slices and top with the remaining slice. Cut each sandwich into quarters and spread the cheese mixture on all four sides of the quarters. Arrange on a baking sheet.

Repeat the process with the remaining bread slices and remaining cheese mixture. Freeze until firm and bake at 350 degrees for 10 minutes.

LAYERED GREEN SALAD

* *

Serves 8

ingredients

1 head lettuce, trimmed
   and chopped
1 rib celery, chopped
1 bell pepper, chopped
Salt and pepper to taste
1 large purple onion, chopped
1 (15-ounce) can tiny peas, drained
2 tablespoons sugar
1 cup mayonnaise
2 cups (8 ounces) shredded
   Cheddar cheese
1 (4-ounce) jar imitation bacon bits

method

Layer the lettuce, celery, bell pepper, salt, pepper, onion, peas, sugar, mayonnaise, cheese and bacon bits in a large flat-bottomed bowl in the order listed. Chill, covered, for 8 to 10 hours before serving.

You may substitute an equal amount of thawed frozen peas for the canned peas.

SPRING PEA SALAD

* *

Fresh spring peas are delicious. If they are scarce, thawed frozen tiny peas may be substituted.

Serves 8

ingredients

1 cup mayonnaise
1/2 cup plain nonfat yogurt
2 cups fresh peas, blanched and
    drained
1 cup dried cherries
3/4 cup chopped pecans
1/2 cup chopped fresh dill weed
4 ribs celery, cut into 1/4-inch pieces
Salt and pepper to taste
1 tablespoon chopped fresh
    dill weed
1 sprig of mint

method

Combine the mayonnaise and yogurt in a bowl and mix well. Fold in the peas, cherries, pecans, 1/2 cup dill weed, celery, salt and pepper. Spoon into a decorative bowl and sprinkle with 1 tablespoon dill weed. Garnish with the mint sprig. Store in the refrigerator until serving time.

FAIRFIELD MARKET CHICKEN SALAD

* *

Makes 2 quarts

ingredients

5 pounds boneless skinless
    chicken breasts
1 cup chopped celery
1/2 cup water chestnuts, chopped
6 tablespoons chopped purple onion
1/4 cup chopped red bell pepper
1/4 cup chopped yellow bell pepper
1 quart (about) mayonnaise
Salt and white pepper to taste
Cayenne pepper to taste

method

Combine the chicken with enough water to cover in a stockpot and bring to a boil. Boil until tender and drain. Cool slightly and shred by hand, discarding any fat.

Combine the shredded chicken, celery, water chestnuts, onion and bell peppers in a bowl and mix well. Add mayonnaise until very moist and mix well. Season to taste with salt, white pepper and cayenne pepper. Store in the refrigerator until serving time.

ORZO AND SHRIMP SALAD

Serves 20

24 ounces orzo

Salt to taste

1 1/2 bunches green onions, trimmed
    and chopped

12 ounces feta cheese, crumbled

3/4 cup chopped fresh dill weed

7 tablespoons fresh lemon juice

6 tablespoons olive oil

3 pounds shrimp, peeled
    and deveined

Pepper to taste

1 1/2 English hothouse cucumbers

2 baskets cherry tomatoes,
    cut into halves

1 cup pine nuts (optional)

1/2 English hothouse cucumber,
    cut into rounds

2 sprigs of dill weed

Cook the pasta in boiling salted water in a saucepan for 10 minutes or just until tender and drain. Rinse with cold water until cool and drain again. Combine the pasta, green onions, cheese, chopped dill weed, lemon juice and olive oil in a bowl and mix well. Cook the shrimp in boiling salted water in a stockpot for 2 minutes or until the shrimp turn pink and drain. Rinse with cold water to cool and drain again. Add to the pasta mixture. Season with salt and pepper. Chill, covered, for up to 8 hours.

Cut 1 1/2 cucumbers lengthwise into quarters and cut crosswise into 1/4-inch pieces. Add the cucumber pieces, three-fourths of the tomatoes and the pine nuts to the pasta mixture and mix well. Spoon the salad into a large serving bowl and arrange the remaining tomatoes and cucumber rounds around the edge of the bowl. Garnish with the sprigs of dill weed.

LEMON DILL NEW POTATOES

Serves 6 to 8

Salt to taste

2 pounds small white or red
    new potatoes

1/4 cup (1/2 stick) unsalted butter

Pepper to taste

Finely grated zest of 2 lemons

6 tablespoons chopped fresh
    dill weed

Bring enough salted water to cover the potatoes to a boil in a stockpot and add the potatoes. Cook for 20 minutes or just until tender and drain.

Toss the hot potatoes with the butter in a large bowl and season generously with salt and pepper. Fold in the lemon zest and 4 tablespoons of the dill weed. Sprinkle with the remaining dill weed.

HOMEMADE SLOPPY JOES

Serves 4 to 6

ingredients

1 pound ground beef or
   veggie crumbles
1/2 cup finely chopped onion
1 cup ketchup
1/2 cup water
1/4 cup packed brown sugar
1 tablespoon white wine vinegar
1 tablespoon prepared mustard
Hamburger buns

method

Brown the ground beef with the onion in a skillet, stirring until the ground beef is crumbly; drain. Mix the ketchup, water, brown sugar, vinegar and prepared mustard in a bowl and stir into the ground beef mixture.

Simmer over low heat for 5 to 10 minutes or until the flavors marry, stirring occasionally. Serve on hamburger buns.

Serve **Ranch French Fries** with Homemade Sloppy Joes. Spray 26 ounces of frozen French fries with nonstick cooking spray and place the potatoes in a sealable plastic bag. Add 1 envelope ranch salad dressing mix and seal tightly. Shake to coat. Spread the potatoes in a single layer on a 10×15-inch baking sheet and bake at 425 degrees for 30 minutes. Stir and bake for 5 to 10 minutes longer or until golden brown.

SKILLET PASTA

Serves 4

ingredients

8 ounces boneless skinless
   chicken breasts
1/4 teaspoon salt
1/4 teaspoon pepper
1 tablespoon olive oil
4 ounces shiitake
   mushrooms, sliced
1 cup heavy cream
1/4 cup crumbled
   Gorgonzola cheese
1/3 cup grated Parmesan cheese
1/4 teaspoon salt
1/4 teaspoon pepper
8 ounces penne, cooked
   and drained
1/4 cup crumbled
   Gorgonzola cheese
2 tablespoons chopped
   fresh parsley

method

Cut the chicken crosswise into 1/2-inch-thick strips. Sprinkle with 1/4 teaspoon salt and 1/4 teaspoon pepper. Heat the olive oil in a nonstick skillet and add the chicken. Cook for 1 1/2 minutes per side or until light brown around the edges. Stir in the mushrooms and cook for 3 minutes or until the mushrooms are tender. Add the heavy cream, 1/4 cup Gorgonzola cheese and the Parmesan cheese gradually, stirring constantly.

Simmer until the cheese melts, stirring frequently. Stir in 1/4 teaspoon salt and 1/4 teaspoon pepper. Toss the chicken mixture with the pasta in a large pasta bowl and sprinkle with 1/4 cup Gorgonzola cheese and the parsley.

BARBECUED SHRIMP

Serves 4

ingredients

1 pound unpeeled large shrimp
1/2 cup (1 stick) butter
1/2 cup bottled chili sauce
Juice of 1 lemon
1 tablespoon Worcestershire sauce
1 teaspoon parsley flakes, or
   1 tablespoon chopped
   fresh parsley
1 teaspoon Tabasco sauce
1/2 teaspoon paprika
2 garlic cloves, crushed
Pepper to taste
1 lemon, thinly sliced

method

Arrange the shrimp in a shallow baking dish. Combine the butter, chili sauce, lemon juice, Worcestershire sauce, parsley flakes, Tabasco sauce, paprika, garlic and pepper in a small saucepan and cook over low heat until heated through, stirring occasionally. Pour over the shrimp and top with the lemon slices.

Chill, covered, for at least 6 hours, turning once or twice. Bake at 325 degrees for 30 minutes, turning with a spatula twice. Serve in soup-size bowls with hot French bread.

CRISPY CATFISH WITH HOMEMADE TARTAR SAUCE

Serves 4

ingredients

HOMEMADE TARTAR SAUCE

1 cup mayonnaise

1 cup sour cream

1 tablespoon lemon pepper

1 tablespoon lemon juice

1 teaspoon dill weed

1 teaspoon minced onion

1/2 teaspoon Old Bay Seasoning

CATFISH

2 tablespoons ranch salad dressing

2 egg whites, lightly beaten

6 tablespoons yellow cornmeal

1/4 cup (1 ounce) grated
   Parmesan cheese

2 tablespoons all-purpose flour

1/4 teaspoon cayenne pepper

1/8 teaspoon salt

4 (6-ounce) catfish fillets

method

SAUCE

Combine the mayonnaise, sour cream, lemon pepper, lemon juice, dill weed, onion and Old Bay Seasoning in a bowl and mix well. Chill, covered, for 2 hours before serving.

CATFISH

Whisk the salad dressing and egg whites in a bowl until combined. Mix the cornmeal, cheese, flour, cayenne pepper and salt in a shallow dish. Dip the fillets in the egg white mixture and coat with the cornmeal mixture.

Arrange the fillets on a baking sheet coated with nonstick cooking spray and bake at 425 degrees for 12 minutes on each side or until the fillets are light brown and flake easily when tested with a fork. Serve with the sauce.

*B*arksdale Air Force Base has proudly served our country and community in Northwest Louisiana for more than seventy years. Construction on Barksdale Field began south of Bossier City in 1931, and it was officially dedicated February 3, 1933. It took about 150 men and 350 mules plowing 1,400 acres of cotton field to create what was once the world's largest airfield. It was later renamed Barksdale Air Force Base and is now home to the "mighty" Eighth Air Force, America's premier bomber command made famous during World War II. Its social and economic impact on Bossier City and Northwest Louisiana is enormous.

MONKEY BREAD

Serves 16

ingredients

3 (10-count) cans buttermilk biscuits
1 cup granulated sugar
2 teaspoons ground cinnamon
1 cup (2 sticks) butter
1/2 cup packed brown sugar

method

Cut each biscuit into quarters. Mix the granulated sugar and cinnamon in a bowl. Coat the biscuit quarters with the granulated sugar mixture and arrange in a buttered bundt pan; do not crowd the pieces.

Combine 1/2 cup of the remaining granulated sugar mixture, the butter and brown sugar in a small saucepan and bring to a boil. Immediately remove from the heat and drizzle the hot mixture over the biscuit pieces. Bake at 350 degrees for 30 minutes. Cool for 5 to 10 minutes and invert onto a serving platter.

DIRT DESSERT

Serves 10 to 12

ingredients

2 (4-ounce) packages vanilla
    instant pudding mix
2 cups milk
8 ounces whipped topping
1 (1-pound) package
    confectioners' sugar
1/2 cup (1 stick) butter, softened
8 ounces cream cheese, softened
1 (20-ounce) package chocolate
    sandwich cookies, crushed
Gummi worms

method

Whisk the pudding mix and milk in a bowl until blended. Fold in the whipped topping. Beat the confectioners' sugar, butter and cream cheese in a mixing bowl until light and fluffy. Fold the cream cheese mixture into the pudding mixture.

Layer one-third of the cookie crumbs and one-half of the pudding mixture in a new eight-inch terra-cotta flowerpot. Top with one-half of the remaining cookie crumbs, the remaining pudding mixture and the remaining cookie crumbs, inserting the gummi worms as desired. Chill in the refrigerator. Just before serving, decorate with silk flowers and serve with a trowel. You may substitute two 6-inch terra-cotta flowerpots or several small terra-cotta flowerpots for the larger flowerpot.

DINOSAUR TOES

An easy dessert that children adore. Take a field trip to a lake, pond, or park, and feed the bread crusts to the ducks, birds, or squirrels.

Makes 40

ingredients

1 (16-ounce) loaf white bread, crusts trimmed
8 ounces cream cheese, softened
1 (8-ounce) can crushed pineapple, drained
1 cup (about) sugar
3/4 to 1 cup (about) ground cinnamon
1/2 to 1 cup (1 to 2 sticks) butter or margarine, melted

method

Using a rolling pin, roll each bread slice on a work surface until flattened. Beat the cream cheese and pineapple in a mixing bowl until combined. Mix the sugar and cinnamon in a bowl.

Spread a heaping spoonful of the cream cheese mixture on each slice of bread and roll tightly to enclose the filling, removing any excess cream cheese mixture that seeps out while rolling. Cut each roll into halves.

Dip each half in the melted butter and coat with the sugar mixture. Arrange on an ungreased baking sheet and bake at 325 degrees for 8 to 12 minutes or until brown and crisp; do not overbake. Cool for 5 minutes. Serve warm or at room temperature. Store, covered, in the refrigerator.

The Junior League celebrated its sixtieth anniversary in 1993. The League honored the community with a gift of $60,000 directed toward the Sci-Port Discovery Center children's exhibit, Kidspace. This gift continues to enhance creativity and curiosity in kids of all ages.

CHOCOLATE PLAY DOUGH

Children love to make and eat this fun food! Makes a great play-date, rainy-day, or party activity.

ingredients

1 (1-pound) package
  confectioners' sugar
1 (4-ounce) package chocolate
  instant pudding mix
1/2 cup peanut butter
1/3 cup margarine, softened
4 to 5 tablespoons milk

method

Combine the confectioners' sugar and pudding mix in a bowl and mix well. Add the peanut butter, margarine and milk and stir until smooth. You can play with this until snack time and then eat your creations. Be sure to wash your hands before you begin, and play on a clean surface.

Try this recipe for **Homemade Play Dough**. Mix 1 cup all-purpose flour, 1/2 cup salt and 2 teaspoons cream of tartar in a saucepan. Stir in 1 cup water, 1 tablespoon vegetable oil and several drops of food coloring. Cook over medium heat until the mixture pulls from the side of the pan, stirring frequently. Remove from the heat and cool just until the mixture can be easily handled. Knead lightly and store in an airtight container or sealable plastic bag.

MAY

During the month of May, proud children

everywhere beam with pride while preparing

breakfast in bed for Mom's special day. And

mudbug madness

before the grip of summer's sweltering heat, our

bonnie and clyde festival

festival season kicks into high gear, celebrating

gusher days

everything from crawfish to outlaws!

poke salad festival

It's a good bet that more mothers eat breakfast in bed on a single day in the month of May than on all of the other days of the year combined. MOTHER'S DAY has been fostering the culinary talents of American children since 1914. Be sure to praise your little chefs…even if, in true Louisiana style, the toast is served blackened.

During the month of May, before the sweltering heat of the Louisiana summer forces the fun either indoors or to the area lakes, our festival season is in full swing. The first full weekend in May sets the pace with a cultural celebration in Logansport called the RIVER CITY FEST. Then the month really gets cookin'.

The largest food festival of the month is the two-day MUDBUG MADNESS in Shreveport, which has been honored by the Southeast Tourism Society. This festival pays tribute to our Cajun heritage with an event complete with Zydeco music, children's activities, arts and crafts, and a crawfish-eating contest. All of this fun is dedicated to the small, red, beady-eyed Louisiana delicacy.

During the third weekend in May, Oil City is home to GUSHER DAYS, a celebration of the historical and cultural significance of the oil industry in Northwest Louisiana. Be sure to visit the Louisiana State Oil and Gas Museum, where even natives may be surprised to find that it was in Oil City in 1904 that the "rich" history of the oil industry as we know it today began. You'll be fascinated to discover that Caddo Lake is actually the birthplace of offshore drilling and that many now-international oil companies got their start right here.

Don't forget to stop by Gibsland this month as the town brings the gruesome ambush of May 23, 1934, back to life at the world's only BONNIE AND CLYDE FESTIVAL. The ambush of the notorious outlaws on Ringgold Road is reenacted every year on the Saturday closest to the anniversary of their death.

The CINCO DE MAYO FESTIVAL in Shreveport fosters solidarity among the Hispanic community with a spirited celebration complete with a Chihuahua dog race, music, food, arts and crafts, and more.

So many other festivals are held in the month of May that it would be impossible to attend them all. Among the notables are the LOGGERS AND FORESTRY FESTIVAL in Zwolle, the POKE SALAD FESTIVAL in Blanchard, the BEEGUM FESTIVAL in Stonewall, the SPRING ARTS FESTIVAL in Minden, and the BENTON ON THE SQUARE HISTORY AND ARTS FESTIVAL.

Whew! Beginning to get a feel for the pace at which Northwest Louisiana celebrates? Keep up, more fun lies ahead.

PINEAPPLE MARGARITA*

ingredients

1/2 cup tequila
1/2 cup pineapple juice
6 tablespoons fresh lime juice
3 tablespoons Triple Sec
2 teaspoons sugar
Crushed ice
Lime slices

*Photograph for this recipe on page 75.

method

Combine the tequila, pineapple juice, lime juice, Triple Sec and sugar in a cocktail shaker. Add crushed ice and shake vigorously until combined. Pour into two margarita glasses and garnish with lime slices. Serve immediately.

MEXICAN SLUSH

Serves about 24

ingredients

7 cups water
2 cups light rum
1 (12-ounce) can frozen lemonade concentrate, thawed
1 (12-ounce) can frozen orange juice concentrate, thawed
2 tablespoons lemon-flavor instant tea granules
3 (2-liter) bottles ginger ale
Maraschino cherries

method

Combine the water, rum, lemonade concentrate, orange juice concentrate and tea granules in a large freezer container and mix until the tea granules dissolve. Freeze, covered, for 8 to 10 hours or until firm.

Let the slush mixture stand at room temperature for 15 minutes. Spoon enough of the slush mixture into glasses to fill halfway and top off with the ginger ale. Garnish with cherries.

CRAWFISH BREAD

Serves 8 to 10

ingredients

1 wide loaf French bread
1 package sliced deli-style
   mozzarella cheese
1/4 cup extra-virgin olive oil
2 tablespoons butter
1 onion, chopped
1 bell pepper, chopped
2 teaspoons minced fresh garlic
1 pound frozen crawfish tails
2 bay leaves
1 1/4 tablespoons Cajun seasoning
2 teaspoons sugar
1/2 teaspoon tarragon
1/16 teaspoon celery salt
4 ounces mild Cheddar
   cheese, shredded
1 package sliced deli-style
   Swiss cheese

method

Cut a horizontal slice from the top of the bread loaf and reserve. Scoop out the center of the loaf, leaving a 1-inch shell. Line the bottom of the shell with 1 layer of the mozzarella cheese. Heat the olive oil and butter in a large skillet until the butter melts and add the onion, bell pepper and garlic. Sauté until the onion is tender and stir in the crawfish tails.

Cook until the crawfish tails begin to wilt. Reduce the heat and stir in the bay leaves, Cajun seasoning, sugar, tarragon and celery salt.

Simmer for 5 to 10 minutes or to the desired consistency, stirring occasionally. Discard the bay leaves and mix in the Cheddar cheese. Pour the crawfish mixture over the mozzarella cheese in the bread shell and layer with the Swiss cheese. Top with the reserved bread top and wrap in foil. Bake at 400 degrees for 10 to 15 minutes. Slice and serve immediately.

In 1980, the Pioneer Heritage Center became a joint project of the Junior League and LSU-Shreveport. The Pioneer Heritage Center comprises seven plantation structures, including the Thrasher House (a log dogtrot) and the Caspiana House (the big house from Caspiana Plantation), both listed on the National Register of Historic Places; a detached kitchen; a log single-pen blacksmith shop; a doctor's office; and a commissary. The structures, exhibits, and artifacts serve as a history laboratory, staffed by Junior League and community volunteers, for students and teachers in the humanities and for community groups, tourists, and the general public.

CRAWFISH CROSTINI

Makes about 30

CROSTINI
1 baguette French bread
Extra-virgin olive oil

CRAWFISH TOPPING
2 tablespoons butter
1/2 cup chopped white onion
1/4 cup chopped celery
1/4 cup chopped green bell pepper
3 garlic cloves, minced
1 pound peeled cooked crawfish tails
1 teaspoon Cajun seasoning, such
   as Bayou Magic
Freshly ground pepper to taste
3/4 cup (3 ounces) shredded
   Parmesan cheese
1/2 cup (2 ounces) shredded
   mozzarella cheese
Tabasco sauce or hot sauce to taste
Shredded Parmesan cheese to taste
2 or 3 green onions, sliced

CROSTINI

Cut the baguette diagonally into 1/4-inch slices. Lightly brush each slice with olive oil and arrange in a single layer on a baking sheet. Toast at 375 degrees for 8 to 10 minutes or until crisp. Remove to a wire rack to cool. Maintain the oven temperature.

TOPPING

Melt the butter in a skillet over medium-low heat and add the onion, celery, bell pepper and garlic. Sauté until the onion is tender. Stir in the crawfish tails, Cajun seasoning and pepper.

Cook for 5 to 10 minutes or until heated through, stirring occasionally. Remove from the heat and stir in 3/4 cup Parmesan cheese, the mozzarella cheese and Tabasco sauce. Spoon 1 heaping tablespoon of the filling on each crostini and sprinkle with Parmesan cheese to taste. Arrange the crostini on a baking sheet and bake for 5 minutes or until the cheese melts and the topping is hot. Remove to a platter and garnish with the green onions.

The River Cities Youth Summit was created by the League in 2003 to serve as a cultural awareness and tolerance training program for middle school students from Caddo and Bossier parishes. Public and private schools were invited to select attending students based on their leadership skills among peers. In recognition for this successful project, the League was awarded the Pete Harris Unity Award by the NCCJ, the National Conference for Community and Justice.

CRAWFISH ELEGANTE

Serve as an hors d'oeuvre in a chafing dish with toast points, or serve at a luncheon in pastry shells.

Makes 1 quart

ingredients

3/4 cup (1 1/2 sticks) butter
1 pound crawfish tails
1 bunch green onions, trimmed
    and chopped
1/2 cup chopped fresh parsley
3 garlic cloves, minced
1/4 cup all-purpose flour
2 cups half-and-half
1 teaspoon Worcestershire sauce
1 teaspoon lemon juice
1/8 teaspoon Tabasco sauce
Salt and cayenne pepper to taste
3 tablespoons sherry

method

Melt 1/4 cup of the butter in a large skillet and add the crawfish tails. Sauté for about 10 minutes, stirring occasionally. Melt the remaining 1/2 cup butter in a large skillet and add the green onions, parsley and garlic. Sauté until the green onions are tender and stir in the flour. Add the half-and-half gradually, stirring constantly.

Cook until thickened, stirring constantly. Add the Worcestershire sauce, lemon juice, Tabasco sauce, salt and cayenne pepper and mix well. Stir in the sautéed crawfish tails. Cook until heated through, stirring occasionally. Just before serving, stir in the sherry and pour into a chafing dish. Serve with toast points or rounds.

MEXICAN CORN BREAD MINI MUFFINS*

Makes 4 dozen muffins

ingredients

1 pound ground beef
1 cup cornmeal
1/2 teaspoon salt
1/2 teaspoon baking soda
1 cup milk
2 eggs
1/2 cup vegetable oil
1 large onion, minced
8 ounces Cheddar cheese, shredded
1 (8-ounce) can cream-style corn
4 jalapeño chiles, seeded
    and chopped

*Photograph for this recipe on page 75.

method

Brown the ground beef in a skillet, stirring until crumbly; drain. Combine the cornmeal, salt and baking soda in a bowl and mix well. Stir in the milk until blended. Add the eggs one at a time, mixing well after each addition. Blend in the oil. Stir in the ground beef, onion, cheese, corn and jalapeño chiles.

Spoon the corn bread mixture into miniature muffin cups sprayed with nonstick cooking spray. Bake at 350 degrees for 12 to 15 minutes or until the muffins test done.

TINY TACO TARTS

ingredients

30 miniature phyllo shells, thawed
3/4 cup mayonnaise
6 tablespoons sour cream
1/4 cup buttermilk
1/2 envelope taco seasoning mix
   (3 tablespoons)
1 tablespoon fresh lime juice
Toppings: grated carrots, shredded
   lettuce, minced cilantro,
   chopped tomato

method

Arrange the phyllo shells on a baking sheet and bake at 375 degrees for 10 minutes or until golden brown. Remove to a wire rack to cool.

Mix the mayonnaise, sour cream, buttermilk, taco seasoning mix and lime juice in a bowl. Fill each phyllo shell with some of the mayonnaise mixture and sprinkle with the desired toppings. Chill, covered, until serving time. For variety, serve as a dip with chunks of fresh vegetables, omitting the phyllo shells.

CORN DIP

ingredients

2 (10-ounce) cans tomatoes with
   green chiles, drained and
   squeezed dry
2 (15-ounce) cans Del Monte fiesta
   corn, drained
2 (4-ounce) cans chopped green
   chiles, drained
2 cups (8 ounces) shredded medium
   Cheddar cheese
3/4 cup fresh cilantro, chopped
1/2 cup finely chopped red
   bell pepper
3 or 4 green onions, chopped
2 jalapeño chiles, seeded and
   chopped
1/2 to 1 cup mayonnaise
1/2 to 1 cup sour cream
Ground cumin to taste
Salt and pepper to taste

method

Combine the tomatoes with green chiles, corn, canned green chiles, cheese, cilantro, bell pepper, green onions and jalapeño chiles in a bowl and mix well. Stir in the mayonnaise and sour cream and season with cumin, salt and pepper. Chill, covered, for up to 24 hours before serving. Serve with corn chip scoops.

Serves 4

ingredients

1/2 cup (1 stick) butter
1 bunch green onions, trimmed
    and chopped
4 to 8 ounces fresh
    mushrooms, sliced
2 garlic cloves, minced
8 ounces cream cheese, cubed
2 (10-ounce) cans cream of
    potato soup
2 (10-ounce) cans niblet corn,
    drained
2 cups half-and-half
1 pound crawfish tails

*Photograph for this recipe on page 75.

method

Melt the butter in a saucepan and add the green onions, mushrooms and garlic. Sauté until the green onions and mushrooms are tender. Add the cream cheese and stir until combined. Stir in the soup, corn, half-and-half and crawfish.

Cook until heated through, stirring occasionally; do not boil. Ladle into soup bowls and serve immediately.

If you have added too much garlic to your soup or stew, add a sprig or small quantity of parsley and simmer for about ten minutes. Rub your hands with salt or a lemon slice to remove garlic odor.

ALMOND MANDARIN SALAD*

Serves 4 to 6

FETA AND ALMOND TOPPING
1/3 cup crumbled feta cheese
1/2 cup sliced almonds
3 tablespoons sugar

BALSAMIC DRESSING
1/4 cup extra-virgin olive oil
2 tablespoons balsamic vinegar
2 tablespoons sugar
1 tablespoon parsley flakes
1 1/2 teaspoons salt
1 1/2 teaspoons pepper
1/4 teaspoon Tabasco sauce

SALAD
1/2 head green leaf lettuce,
   trimmed and torn
1/2 head red leaf lettuce,
   trimmed and torn
1 (11-ounce) can mandarin
   oranges, drained
1 cup chopped celery
1/2 cup dried cranberries
2 green onions, chopped

*Photograph for this recipe on page 75.

TOPPING
Toss the feta cheese, almonds and sugar in a baking pan and broil until the sugar melts, stirring occasionally. Let stand until cool.

DRESSING
Combine the olive oil, vinegar, sugar, parsley flakes, salt, pepper and Tabasco sauce in a jar with a tight-fitting lid and seal tightly. Shake until the sugar and salt dissolve.

SALAD
Toss the lettuce, mandarin oranges, celery, cranberries and green onions in a salad bowl. Add the dressing and mix until coated. Sprinkle with the topping.

The Mollie E. Webb Speech and Hearing Center was created by the Junior League in 1973 after studies established a need for a comprehensive facility for treatment and diagnostic services for children and adults with speech or hearing impairments and other communicative disorders.

CAJUN PASTA SALAD

Serves 6 to 8

ingredients

HERBED DRESSING

3 tablespoons minced fresh herbs
   (parsley, chives, basil)
Juice of 1/2 lemon
Juice of 1/2 lime
1 tablespoon vinegar
1 tablespoon prepared mustard
1 teaspoon salt
1/8 teaspoon Tabasco sauce
Yolks of 2 hard-cooked eggs
1 egg yolk
1 1/2 cups vegetable oil

SALAD

12 ounces tri-color rotini
Salt to taste
1/4 cup vegetable oil
1 pound crawfish tails
1 cup chopped onion
2 garlic cloves, minced
1 small jalapeño chile, seeded
   and minced
1 tomato, chopped
1 cup chopped celery
1 cup chopped water chestnuts
1 cup sliced black olives
1 cup chopped red bell pepper
Whites of 2 hard-cooked eggs,
   chopped
1 tablespoon rinsed drained capers
Pepper to taste

method

DRESSING

Process the herbs, lemon juice, lime juice, vinegar, prepared mustard, salt and Tabasco sauce in a blender until puréed. Add the hard-cooked egg yolks and raw egg yolk. Add the oil gradually, processing constantly until the oil is incorporated. If you are concerned about using raw egg yolks, use yolks from eggs pasteurized in their shells, which are sold at some specialty food stores, or use an equivalent amount of pasteurized egg substitute.

SALAD

Cook the pasta in boiling salted water in a saucepan until al dente. Drain and toss with 2 tablespoons of the oil in a bowl. Heat the remaining 2 tablespoons oil in a skillet and add the crawfish tails, onion, garlic and jalapeño chile. Sauté until the onion and crawfish are tender.

Toss the pasta, crawfish mixture, tomato, celery, water chestnuts, olives, bell pepper, egg whites and capers in a bowl. Add the dressing and mix gently until coated. Season with salt and pepper. Chill, covered, until serving time.

ingredients

1 pound ground chuck

1 (14- to 16-ounce) can diced
  tomatoes, drained

1/2 cup salsa or picante sauce

1 envelope taco seasoning mix

1 (2-ounce) can French-fried onions

1 1/2 cups cottage cheese

2 cups (8 ounces) shredded sharp
  Cheddar cheese, divided

2 eggs, lightly beaten

8 to 12 (6-inch) corn or flour tortillas

Toppings: shredded lettuce, chopped
  tomatoes, sliced olives, sour
  cream and/or salsa (optional)

method

Brown the ground chuck in a skillet, stirring until crumbly; drain. Stir in the diced tomatoes, 1/2 cup salsa and the taco seasoning mix. Simmer for 5 minutes, stirring occasionally. Add one-half of the onions and mix well. Combine the cottage cheese, 1 cup Cheddar cheese and the eggs in a bowl and mix well.

Arrange 2 or 3 of the tortillas over the bottom of a 9×13-inch baking dish sprayed with nonstick cooking spray and overlap 4 to 6 of the remaining tortillas around the sides. Spoon the ground chuck mixture into the prepared baking dish and top with 2 or 3 of the remaining tortillas. Spread the cheese mixture over the top and cover with foil.

Bake at 350 degrees for 45 minutes and remove the foil. Sprinkle with the remaining 1 cup Cheddar cheese and the remaining onions. Bake, uncovered, for 5 minutes longer. Top each serving with the desired toppings.

You may assemble in advance and store, covered, in the refrigerator. Add 10 minutes to the first baking time.

JALAPEÑO CHICKEN

Serves 6 to 8

ingredients

1/4 cup (1/2 stick) butter
1 cup chopped onion
3 large or medium boneless skinless
   chicken breasts, cooked and
   chopped into bite-size pieces
2 (10-ounce) cans cream of
   chicken soup
2 cups sour cream
1 (10-ounce) package frozen
   chopped broccoli, cooked and
   drained
4 green onions, trimmed
   and chopped
2 jalapeño chiles, membranes
   removed, seeded and chopped
2 teaspoons salt
4 ounces corn chips
8 ounces Monterey Jack
   cheese, shredded

method

Melt the butter in a 3-quart saucepan and add the onion. Sauté until tender but not brown. Stir in the chicken, soup, sour cream, broccoli, green onions, jalapeño chiles and salt.

Arrange the chips over the bottom of a greased 9×13-inch baking dish and spread the chicken mixture over the chips. Bake at 350 degrees for 1 hour and sprinkle with the cheese. Bake until the cheese melts. Serve with hot crusty French bread or additional chips and salad.

Be sure to wear gloves when working with jalapeño chiles. The heat from the chiles is known to burn the skin and eyes.

CRAWFISH BOIL*

Variable servings

3 (4-ounce) jars crab boil
   concentrate
6 pouches shrimp and crab boil
1/2 cup cayenne pepper
2 bell peppers, quartered
2 ribs celery
3 boxes salt
6 garlic cloves, sliced across the
   grain into halves
4 large onions
1 to 3 new potatoes per guest
1 to 2 ears of corn per guest
1 to 2 pounds crawfish per guest

*Photograph for this recipe on page 75.

Fill a large stockpot one-fourth of the way with water. Add the crab boil concentrate, shrimp and crab boil, cayenne pepper, bell peppers, celery, salt, garlic, onions, new potatoes and corn and bring to a boil.

Purge the crawfish and add the crawfish to the stockpot. Return to a boil and boil for 5 minutes. Let stand for 20 minutes. Drain, discarding the shrimp and crab boil, bell peppers, celery and onions.

To easily remove the meat from crawfish, gently twist off the tail away from the body; then unwrap the first three sections of the shell to expose the meat. Next, hold the end of the meat with one hand while pinching the tail in the other hand to pull the meat out in one piece. If you wish, you can also suck out the flavorful juices from the head.

CREAMY CRAWFISH PASTA*

Serves 6 to 8

16 ounces linguini

1/2 cup (1 stick) butter

1/3 cup all-purpose flour

1 bunch green onions, trimmed and
    finely chopped

1 small onion, minced

4 garlic cloves, minced

1/2 green bell pepper, chopped

2 ribs celery, chopped

1 chicken bouillon cube

2 pounds frozen crawfish tails,
    thawed

2 cups heavy cream

1 (10-ounce) can tomatoes with
    green chiles, drained

1 tablespoon Creole seasoning

1 tablespoon chopped fresh parsley

1/4 teaspoon pepper

1/8 teaspoon salt

Hot sauce to taste

Grated Parmesan cheese (optional)

*Photograph for this recipe on page 75.

Cook the pasta using the package directions and drain. Cover to keep warm. Melt the butter in a Dutch oven over medium heat and stir in the flour. Cook for 2 minutes or until smooth and bubbly, stirring constantly. Add the green onions, small onion, garlic, bell pepper and celery and mix well.

Sauté for 5 minutes or until the vegetables are tender. Add the bouillon cube, crawfish tails, heavy cream, tomatoes with green chiles, Creole seasoning, parsley, pepper and salt and mix well. Cook for 10 minutes or until thickened, stirring occasionally. Stir in hot sauce and spoon the crawfish mixture over the pasta on a serving platter. Sprinkle with Parmesan cheese and serve immediately.

CHIPOTLE PRAWNS WITH GOAT CHEESE POLENTA

This recipe comes from Chef Steven Alex Vanderpool of Bella Fresca

Serves 4 to 6

ingredients

PRAWNS AND CHIPOTLE MARINADE

12 to 18 prawns

1 (7-ounce) can chipotle chiles in adobo sauce

1 cup canola oil

8 garlic cloves

1/2 small onion, chopped

1/3 cup sugar

Juice of 3 limes

1/4 bunch cilantro, trimmed

GOAT CHEESE POLENTA

4 cups water

2 1/2 cups milk

1 pound cornmeal polenta

1/2 cup (1 stick) butter

8 ounces goat cheese

Salt and pepper to taste

SAUZA TEQUILA LIME BUTTER AND ASSEMBLY

1 teaspoon canola oil

1 teaspoon minced garlic

1 teaspoon minced onion

1/2 jalapeño chile, seeded and minced

2 shots of Sauza tequila

Juice of 1 lime

1 teaspoon chopped fresh cilantro

1 cup (2 sticks) butter, cubed

Salt and pepper to taste

1 sprig of cilantro

method

PRAWNS

Clean and devein the prawns, leaving the heads on. Combine the undrained chipotle chiles, canola oil, garlic, onion, sugar, lime juice and cilantro in a food processor or blender and process for 1 minute or until smooth. Combine the prawns with 1/2 cup of the marinade in a shallow dish and turn to coat. Marinate in the refrigerator for 2 hours. Store the remaining marinade in the refrigerator for up to 2 weeks.

POLENTA

Bring the water and milk to a boil in a large heavy saucepan and reduce the heat to low. Add the cornmeal gradually, whisking constantly. Remove from the heat and stir in the butter and then the goat cheese. Season with salt and pepper. Cover to keep warm. Serves four to six.

BUTTER

Heat the canola oil in a small saucepan over medium heat and stir in the garlic, onion and jalapeño chile. Sauté until the onion is tender. Add 1 shot of the tequila, the lime juice and chopped cilantro and cook for 1 minute, stirring frequently. Whisk in the butter until combined and remove from the heat. Season with salt and pepper and cover to keep warm. Consume the remaining 1 shot of tequila.

ASSEMBLY

Grill the prawns over hot coals for 3 minutes on each side or until cooked through. Spoon the polenta into a large bowl and top with the prawns. Drizzle with the desired amount of sauce and garnish with the sprig of cilantro.

MEXICAN CHEW BREAD

The flavor reminds you of the top of a pecan pie. This makes an easy after-school snack.

Makes 24 bars

ingredients

1 (1-pound) package light
   brown sugar
4 eggs, lightly beaten
2 cups all-purpose flour
1 cup pecans
1 teaspoon vanilla extract
1/2 teaspoon salt

method

Combine the brown sugar and eggs in a saucepan and mix well. Cook until the brown sugar melts, stirring frequently. Beat until foamy and remove from the heat. Add the flour, pecans, vanilla and salt and mix until combined.

Spread the brown sugar mixture on a 10×15-inch baking sheet and bake at 400 degrees for 10 to 15 minutes or until brown. Let stand until cool and cut into bars.

CREAM CHEESE SQUARES

Makes 2 to 3 dozen squares

ingredients

2 (8-count) cans crescent rolls
16 ounces cream cheese, softened
3/4 cup granulated sugar
1 egg yolk
2 teaspoons lemon juice
1 teaspoon vanilla extract
1 egg white, lightly beaten
Confectioners' sugar to taste
Ground cinnamon to taste

method

Spread 1 can of crescent rolls over the bottom of a 9×13-inch baking dish, sealing the ends and perforations to cover. Beat the cream cheese, granulated sugar, egg yolk, lemon juice and vanilla in a mixing bowl until blended.

Spread the cream cheese mixture over the prepared layer and top with the remaining can of crescent roll dough. Brush the top with the egg white and bake at 350 degrees for 20 to 25 minutes or until golden brown. Chill slightly and dust with confectioners' sugar and cinnamon. Cut into squares. Store in the refrigerator.

Serves 12

CAKE
1 (2-layer) package yellow cake mix
1/3 cup peanut butter
1/3 cup vegetable oil
3 eggs
1 teaspoon vanilla extract
1 1/3 cups water

PEANUT BUTTER FROSTING AND ASSEMBLY
38 bite-size peanut butter cups
1/4 cup (1/2 stick) butter, softened
1/4 cup peanut butter
4 cups (or more) confectioners' sugar
1/2 cup warm milk
2 teaspoons vanilla extract

*Photograph for this recipe on page 75.

CAKE
Combine the cake mix, peanut butter, oil, eggs and vanilla in a large mixing bowl. Add the water and beat until blended. Divide the batter evenly among three lightly greased and floured 9-inch cake pans. Bake at 350 degrees for 18 to 20 minutes or until the layers test done. Cool in the cake pans for 10 minutes and remove to a wire rack to cool completely.

FROSTING
Freeze the peanut butter cups for 15 minutes. Finely chop 28 of the cups. Beat the butter and peanut butter in a mixing bowl until creamy. Add 2 cups of the confectioners' sugar, 1/4 cup of the warm milk and the vanilla and beat until blended. Add the remaining 2 cups confectioners' sugar and remaining 1/4 cup warm milk and beat until thickened and fluffy, adding additional confectioners' sugar if needed for the desired consistency.

ASSEMBLY
Place one of the cake layers on a cake plate and spread with frosting to cover. Sprinkle with one-half of the chopped peanut butter cups and top with another cake layer. Spread with frosting and sprinkle with the remaining chopped peanut butter cups. Top with the remaining cake layer and spread the remaining frosting over the top and side of the cake. Arrange the remaining 10 whole peanut butter cups on the top of the cake in a decorative pattern. Store, covered, at room temperature for 1 day, or in the refrigerator, covered, for up to 4 days.

JUNE

With the kids out of school and the celebration

of Father's Day, June is a great month for

sunflower trail and festival

spending time with the family at one of our

squire creek peach festival

many summer festivals. From sunflowers and

louisiana blueberry festival

peaches to blueberries and black-eyed peas,

melrose arts and crafts festival

Northwest Louisiana celebrates it all!

*M*ost kids are out of school by now, and families are spending more time together, so June is a great month to celebrate summer's arrival as a family. It also happens to be the month we celebrate another important member of the family, Dad. The idea of a national Father's Day was supported as early as 1924, but it wasn't until 1966 that a proclamation was signed declaring the third Sunday in June as FATHER'S DAY.

What better way to spend time together than by driving down the scenic and historic SUNFLOWER TRAIL to the SUNFLOWER FESTIVAL in Gilliam? This festival features regional artists, food booths, hands-on arts and crafts for children, and entertainment under the trees behind the Crossroads Museum on the last Saturday of the month.

Take a step back into the antebellum history of Louisiana at the ANNUAL MELROSE ARTS AND CRAFTS FESTIVAL, held each year on the second weekend in June on the beautiful grounds of the historic Melrose Plantation. It is considered to be the oldest arts and crafts show in Louisiana, with more than thirty years of celebrations and counting. Each year more than one hundred artisans from throughout the south travel to Melrose Plantation to display their items. Festival activities include guided tours of Melrose's Main House and the African House, as well as a sampling of true Louisiana cuisine.

Our rich culture and history gives plenty of reasons for celebrations, but food is a common theme. For example, you can pack up the family and head to Ruston for the annual SQUIRE CREEK LOUISIANA PEACH FESTIVAL, a Lincoln Parish favorite since 1951. The festival opens in early June and reaches a crescendo with a spectacular parade on the Saturday before Father's Day. This multi-day event has activities for nearly every taste, including sporting events, a street dance, outdoor concerts, a fine arts exhibit, and a rodeo. And, of course, there's also a peach-eating contest.

If it's blueberries you prefer, make your way to Mansfield at the end of the month to attend the annual LOUISIANA BLUEBERRY FESTIVAL. This event honors the life's work of a couple who started by planting two acres of blueberries in DeSoto Parish roughly twenty-five years ago, sparking an industry that now produces a million pounds of blueberries per year. At this celebration, you will naturally find everything blueberry, from drinks, syrups, and popsicles to butter, breads, and pies. If you feel creative, enter the baking contest to see how your recipe fares.

THE BLACK-EYED PEA FESTIVAL in Bossier City celebrates Juneteenth, the oldest nationally celebrated commemoration of the ending of slavery in the United States. This local festival is a neighborhood event on Hamilton Road in Bossier City. Festivities include church choirs, children's entertainment, and bowls full of black-eyed peas.

With generally favorable weather, June is an excellent month for outdoor festivals, and though deciding which one to attend may not be easy, it's sure to be a sweet decision.

CHICKEN BACON BITES WITH APRICOT SAUCE

Makes 2 dozen chicken bites

ingredients

APRICOT DIPPING SAUCE
1/2 cup apricot preserves
2 tablespoons balsamic vinegar
1 tablespoon soy sauce

CHICKEN BITES
2 large boneless skinless
    chicken breasts
8 slices bacon, cut into thirds
1/2 cup apricot preserves
1/4 cup soy sauce
2 tablespoons sesame oil
1 teaspoon ground ginger
1 garlic clove, minced

method

SAUCE
Combine the preserves, vinegar and soy sauce in a bowl and mix well.

CHICKEN BITES
Cut the chicken into twenty-four 1-inch cubes. Wrap each chicken cube with 1 bacon slice and secure with a wooden pick.

Combine the preserves, soy sauce, sesame oil, ginger and garlic in a shallow dish or sealable plastic bag and add the chicken. Cover or seal tightly and marinate in the refrigerator for 2 hours, turning occasionally.

Coat a broiler rack with nonstick cooking spray and arrange the chicken bites on the prepared rack. Place the rack in a broiler pan and bake at 450 degrees for 10 minutes. Turn the chicken bites and bake for 10 minutes longer. Serve warm with the sauce.

BLUEBERRY SALSA

Makes 3 cups

ingredients

2 cups fresh blueberries, chopped
1 cup fresh whole blueberries
1/3 cup chopped red bell pepper
1/4 cup chopped onion
1/4 cup fresh lemon juice
3 tablespoons chopped fresh cilantro
2 jalapeño chiles, seeded
   and minced
1/2 teaspoon salt

method

Combine the chopped blueberries, whole blueberries, bell pepper, onion, lemon juice, cilantro, jalapeño chiles and salt in a bowl and mix gently. Chill, covered, in the refrigerator until serving time.

Do not rinse blueberries until you are ready to use them. If you happen to have more blueberries than you can use immediately, spread the additional blueberries in a single layer on a baking sheet and freeze. This prevents the blueberries from sticking together. Store the frozen blueberries in a sealable freezer bag for future use. This method works for most fresh berries.

ASIAN SLAW

*Any slaw mix can be used in this extremely versatile dish. Broccoli slaw and angel hair
slaw are the most commonly used slaw mixes.*

Serves 8 to 10

ingredients

2 (3-ounce) packages beef-flavor
  ramen noodles
1 (11-ounce) package slaw mix
1 cup sliced almonds
1 cup sunflower seeds
1 bunch green onions, chopped
3/4 cup vegetable oil
1/2 cup sugar
1/3 cup salad vinegar

method

Reserve the flavor packets from the noodles.
Crush the noodles and arrange in the bottom of
a salad bowl. Layer the slaw mix, almonds,
sunflower seeds and green onions in the order
listed over the noodles.

Whisk the contents of the reserved flavor
packets, oil, sugar and vinegar in a bowl until
blended and pour over the prepared layers; do
not stir. Chill, covered, for 24 hours. Stir just
before serving. You may store the slaw in the
refrigerator for several days.

GREEN SALAD WITH TARRAGON VINAIGRETTE

Serves 8

ingredients

TARRAGON VINAIGRETTE
1/2 cup vegetable oil
1/4 cup tarragon wine vinegar
1/4 cup sugar
1/2 teaspoon salt
1/4 teaspoon pepper
1/4 teaspoon hot sauce

SALAD
1 head Boston lettuce, curly endive
  or leaf lettuce, torn
1 small purple onion, chopped
1/4 cup coarsely chopped
  pecans, toasted

method

VINAIGRETTE
Combine the oil, vinegar, sugar, salt, pepper and
hot sauce in a jar with a tight-fitting lid and seal
tightly. Shake to blend.

SALAD
Toss the lettuce, onion and pecans in a salad
bowl. Add the vinaigrette and mix until coated.

RICE AND PEACH SALAD

Serves 10

ingredients

1½ cups cooked instant brown rice

1 (11-ounce) can whole kernel
  corn, drained

1 cup almonds, toasted
  and chopped

1 cup fresh peas or thawed
  frozen peas

1 peach, peeled and
  coarsely chopped

¼ cup chopped red onion

¼ cup chopped fresh cilantro
  or parsley

½ cup Catalina salad dressing

method

Combine the brown rice, corn, almonds, peas, peach, onion and cilantro in a bowl and mix well. Add the salad dressing and stir until coated. Chill, covered, in the refrigerator until serving time.

NEW POTATOES ON ROSEMARY SKEWERS

Serves 6

ingredients

6 woody rosemary branches

8 red potatoes

Olive oil

1 envelope ranch salad
  dressing mix

method

Remove all the sprigs from the rosemary branches except for a few at the top. Blanch the potatoes in boiling water in a saucepan for 10 minutes or just until tender. Drain and let stand until cool.

Cut the potatoes into quarters and thread on the rosemary skewers. Drizzle with olive oil and sprinkle with the dressing mix. Grill over hot coals until brown, crisp and tender, turning occasionally.

CRISP SWEET POTATO WEDGES

··

Serve with Pulled Pork with Peaches on page 99.

Serves 4

Serve with Pulled Pork with Peaches on page 99.

ingredients

4 sweet potatoes, cut into wedges
1 tablespoon canola oil
1/2 teaspoon paprika
1/4 teaspoon freshly ground pepper
1/8 teaspoon salt

method

Combine the sweet potatoes with enough ice water to cover in a bowl. Let stand, covered, for 15 minutes and drain. Spread the sweet potatoes on double layers of paper towels and press to release any excess moisture.

Place the sweet potatoes in a large bowl and drizzle with the canola oil. Sprinkle with the paprika, pepper and salt and arrange the sweet potato wedges in a single layer on a baking sheet sprayed with nonstick cooking spray. Bake at 425 degrees for 20 minutes and turn. Bake for 20 minutes longer or until golden brown.

The surface of a cut potato deteriorates very quickly when exposed to air. When this occurs, a layer of sticky starch forms as soon as the potatoes are placed in oil. The potatoes may stick to each other, as well as to the pan, making them hard to serve. Soaking potatoes in water for five to seven minutes before frying them will remove most of the surface starch.

VEGETABLE PIES

Serves 12 to 16

ingredients

1/4 cup (1/2 stick) butter

1 large onion, coarsely chopped

2 zucchini, sliced

2 yellow squash, sliced

1 large bell pepper, cut into
   large pieces

2 garlic cloves, minced

Salt and pepper to taste

2 tomatoes, chopped

2 (9- or 10-inch) unbaked pie shells

1 cup mayonnaise

1 cup (4 ounces) shredded
   mozzarella cheese

method

Melt the butter in a large skillet and add the onion, zucchini, yellow squash, bell pepper, garlic, salt and pepper. Sauté until the vegetables are tender-crisp and drain well. Arrange the tomatoes evenly over the bottom of the pie shells and top evenly with the sautéed vegetables.

Mix the mayonnaise and cheese in a bowl and spread over the prepared layers. Bake at 325 degrees for 1 to 1 1/4 hours. If needed to prevent the crust from overbrowning, cover the pies loosely with foil shiny side up. You may freeze for future use.

PULLED PORK WITH PEACHES

Serves 12

ingredients

1 (5-pound) boneless pork roast,
   or 5 pounds pork tenderloins

4 cups sliced peeled fresh peaches,
   or 2 (16-ounce) cans
   peaches, drained

1 cup packed brown sugar

2/3 cup ketchup

2/3 cup white wine vinegar

1/4 cup soy sauce

2 tablespoons minced garlic

method

Cook the pork in a slow cooker on Low for 5 hours. Remove the pork and shred with two forks. Discard the cooking liquids and return the pork to the slow cooker. Combine the peaches, brown sugar, ketchup, vinegar, soy sauce and garlic in a blender and process until puréed. Add the peach purée to the pork and mix well. Cook on Low for 1 to 2 hours longer. You may freeze for future use.

PORK SHISH KABOBS

A beautiful and colorful entrée for outdoor entertaining. Complete the meal with a green salad, wild rice, and crusty French bread.

Serves 6 to 8

ingredients

MARINADE
½ cup vegetable oil
2 tablespoons red wine vinegar
1 tablespoon Dijon mustard
1 garlic clove, minced
1 teaspoon salt
½ teaspoon pepper

PORK KABOBS
2 pounds boneless pork
   chops, cubed
Small whole onions
Green, red and/or yellow bell
   peppers, cut into chunks
Whole mushrooms
Cherry tomatoes

method

MARINADE
Whisk the oil, vinegar, Dijon mustard, garlic, salt and pepper in a bowl until blended.

KABOBS
Pour the marinade over the pork in a sealable plastic bag and seal tightly. Shake to coat. Marinate in the refrigerator for 4 to 10 hours, turning occasionally.

Parboil the onions and bell peppers, if desired. Drain the pork, reserving the marinade. Thread the pork, onions, bell peppers, mushrooms and tomatoes alternately on skewers. Grill over medium heat until the pork is cooked through, turning occasionally and basting with the reserved marinade during the early stages of the grilling process. You may broil the kabobs, if desired.

*B*amboo skewers and wooden picks are an inexpensive and popular way to cook meat on the grill. They should be soaked in water for thirty minutes before grilling. The water prevents the skewers from burning in all but the highest of heat. This is not necessary if the skewers are soaked in the marinade with the meat.

GREEK CHICKEN KABOBS

* *

Serve with a Greek salad of mixed greens, feta cheese, tomatoes, black olives
and a vinaigrette dressing, brown rice, hummus, and pita bread.
Serves 4 to 6

ingredients

MARINADE
1/2 cup extra-virgin olive oil
1/3 cup red wine vinegar
Juice of 1 lemon
4 garlic cloves, minced
1 teaspoon oregano
1/2 teaspoon kosher salt
1/4 teaspoon freshly ground pepper

CHICKEN KABOBS
2 pounds boneless skinless chicken
   breasts, cut into 1-inch pieces
1 yellow bell pepper, cut into
   1-inch pieces
1 green bell pepper, cut into
   1-inch pieces
1 red onion, cut into 1-inch pieces
8 ounces whole button mushrooms
   or cremini mushrooms

method

MARINADE
Whisk the olive oil, vinegar, lemon juice, garlic, oregano, salt and pepper in a bowl until combined.

KABOBS
Pour the marinade over the chicken in a nonreactive bowl and mix well. Marinate, covered, in the refrigerator for 4 hours or longer, stirring occasionally. Drain the chicken, reserving the marinade.

Thread the chicken, bell peppers, onion and mushrooms alternately on skewers and brush with the reserved marinade. Grill over medium to medium-high heat for 15 to 20 minutes or until the chicken is cooked through and the vegetables are tender, turning occasionally.

SALMON WITH PEACH JAM

Serves 4

ingredients

4 (6-ounce) salmon fillets
1/4 teaspoon salt
1/4 cup peach jam
2 tablespoons soy sauce
2 garlic cloves, minced

method

Line a broiler rack with foil and place in a broiler pan. Arrange the fillets on the foil and sprinkle evenly with the salt. Mix the jam, soy sauce and garlic in a bowl and spread one-half of the peach mixture over the fillets.

Bake at 400 degrees for 18 minutes or until the fillets flake easily when tested with a fork. Remove from the oven and spread the fillets with the remaining peach mixture. Broil for 3 minutes or until brown.

DIJON SHRIMP

Serves 3 to 4

ingredients

1 pound medium to large shrimp
1/2 cup (1 stick) butter, melted
2 tablespoons vegetable oil
Juice of 1 lemon
2 tablespoons Dijon mustard
1/2 teaspoon Worcestershire sauce
2 garlic cloves, chopped

method

Peel and devein the shrimp, leaving the tails intact. Place the shrimp in a 9×13-inch baking dish. Whisk the butter, oil, lemon juice, Dijon mustard, Worcestershire sauce and garlic in a bowl and pour over the shrimp, turning to coat.

Marinate, covered, in the refrigerator for 2 to 3 hours, turning occasionally. Broil the undrained shrimp for 5 to 8 minutes or until the shrimp turn pink.

BLUEBERRY SAUSAGE BREAKFAST CAKE

Serves 15

BREAKFAST CAKE

2 cups all-purpose flour
1 teaspoon baking powder
1/2 teaspoon baking soda
1/2 cup (1 stick) butter or margarine
3/4 cup granulated sugar
1/4 cup packed brown sugar
2 eggs
1 cup sour cream
1 pound sausage, cooked
 and drained
1 cup blueberries
1/2 cup chopped pecans

BLUEBERRY SAUCE

1/2 cup sugar
2 tablespoons cornstarch
2 cups fresh or frozen blueberries
1/2 cup water
1/2 teaspoon lemon juice

CAKE

Mix the flour, baking powder and baking soda together. Beat the butter in a mixing bowl at medium to high speed until light and fluffy. Add the granulated sugar and brown sugar and beat until smooth. Add the eggs one at a time, beating for 1 minute after each addition. Add the flour mixture alternately with the sour cream, beating just until combined after each addition. Fold in the sausage and blueberries.

Spoon the batter into an ungreased 9×13-inch baking pan and sprinkle with the pecans. You may cover and chill at this point for 8 to 10 hours, if desired. Bake at 350 degrees for 35 to 40 minutes or until a wooden pick inserted in the center comes out clean. Store leftovers in the refrigerator.

SAUCE

Mix the sugar and cornstarch in a saucepan. Stir in the blueberries and water and cook over medium heat until thickened, stirring constantly. Cook for 2 minutes longer, stirring constantly. Stir in the lemon juice and cool slightly. Serve with the warm cake. Store leftovers in the refrigerator.

*F*irst Lady Eleanor Roosevelt delivered two addresses in 1937 at the Municipal Auditorium in Shreveport.

BLUEBERRY BREAD PUDDING

Serves 10 to 12

ingredients

1 loaf French bread, cubed

8 ounces cream cheese, cubed

1 cup blueberries

4 cups milk

6 eggs

1/2 cup sugar

1/4 cup (1/2 stick) butter, melted

2 cups blueberries

1 (10-ounce) jar 100% fruit
   blackberry jelly

method

Arrange one-half of the bread cubes in a 9×13-inch baking dish. Sprinkle with the cream cheese and 1 cup blueberries and top with the remaining bread cubes. Whisk the milk, eggs, sugar and butter in a bowl until blended and pour over the prepared layers.

Chill, covered, for 8 to 10 hours. Bake, covered, at 350 degrees for 30 minutes. Remove the cover and bake for 30 minutes longer. Let stand for 5 minutes before serving. Heat 2 cups blueberries and the jelly in a saucepan over low heat until the jelly melts, stirring occasionally. Let stand for 20 minutes and serve with the warm bread pudding.

BAKED PEACH FRENCH TOAST

Serves 5 to 7

ingredients

10 to 14 slices French bread,
   1 inch thick

3 ounces cream cheese, softened

1 or 2 (9-ounce) cans sliced
   peaches, drained

1/4 cup chopped pecans

1 cup milk

1/3 cup maple syrup

3 eggs

2 tablespoons butter, melted

1 tablespoon sugar

1 teaspoon ground cinnamon

1 teaspoon vanilla extract

method

Spread both sides of the bread slices with the cream cheese and arrange in a single layer in a 9×13-inch baking pan. Pierce the slices several times with a fork. Layer with the peaches and pecans.

Whisk the milk, syrup, eggs, butter, sugar, cinnamon and vanilla in a bowl until blended and pour over the prepared layers. Bake at 400 degrees for 20 to 25 minutes or until set. You may substitute 3 or 4 sliced large peaches for the canned peaches.

CAMBRIDGE CLUB'S BLUEBERRY APPLE PIE

Serves 6 to 8

ingredients

PIE

1 unbaked (9-inch) pie shell
2 egg whites, lightly beaten
2 cups milk
1/3 cup honey
5 egg yolks
1/4 cup cornstarch
10 envelopes Splenda
3 Granny Smith apples, peeled and
   coarsely chopped
1 cup fresh or frozen blueberries
Grated zest and juice of 1 lemon
1/4 cup water
3/4 cup plain yogurt

TOPPING

2 cups heavy whipping cream
5 envelopes Splenda
1 tablespoon vanilla extract

method

PIE

Pierce the pie shell with a fork and brush with the egg whites. Bake at 325 degrees for 12 to 15 minutes or until golden brown. Cool on a wire rack. Combine the milk and honey in a saucepan and bring just to a boil. Remove from the heat. Whisk the egg yolks, cornstarch and Splenda in a heatproof bowl until blended. Stir some of the hot milk mixture into the egg yolk mixture; then stir the egg yolk mixture into the milk mixture. Cook over medium heat until the first bubbles appear, stirring constantly. Remove from the heat and let stand until cool. Mix the apples, blueberries, lemon zest, lemon juice and water in a saucepan and cook over low heat for 15 minutes, stirring occasionally; do not overcook. Remove from the heat and let stand until cool. Fold the apple mixture into the milk mixture. Fold in the yogurt. Spoon into the baked pie shell and chill for 2 hours or longer.

TOPPING

Beat the ingredients in a mixing bowl until firm peaks form. Spread over the pie filling. Store, covered, in the refrigerator until serving time.

*B*uilt in 1912 amongst majestic oaks, The Cambridge Club of Shreveport was originally the Palmer family residence in the historic Highland District. In 1955, the League bought the house, which served as its headquarters for seventeen years. The house was sold in 1972 to the late Joe Corrente and his wife, Lumen. The Campanellas purchased the property in 1982 and thus began the Cambridge Club of Shreveport. Greg and Patti Carey purchased the Cambridge Club in 2001, and they carry on a twenty-plus-year tradition that consistently offers its members the highest of standards in service and cuisine.

SHUQUALAK FARMS BLUEBERRY POPSICLES

Makes about 20 popsicles

ingredients

Blueberries
2¹/₂ cups water
2 cups sugar
1 cup lemonade mix

method

Crush enough blueberries to measure 4 cups. Combine the crushed blueberries and water in a saucepan and bring to a boil. Reduce the heat to low and simmer, covered, for 3 to 4 minutes. Drain in a colander. Place the colander over a bowl and press the blueberries to extract the juice. Strain the juice, discarding the solids.

Combine 3 cups of the blueberry juice and the sugar in a saucepan and mix well. Bring to a rolling boil and remove from the heat. Let stand until cool. Stir in the lemonade mix and pour into a 1-gallon container. Add enough water to fill to the top and stir. Pour the blueberry mixture into popsicle molds and freeze until firm. You may use sugar-free lemonade mix, if desired.

*S*huqualak Farms in Frierson, Louisiana, is a berry lover's paradise. The acres of blueberry and blackberry bushes, complete with a pond, towering oak trees, and picnic tables, provide a rural and relaxing escape. Harnesses, buckets, bags, and Blueberry Popsicles are provided to make picking comfortable and convenient.

HONEY BARS

Makes 2 to 3 dozen bars

ingredients

BARS

2 cups all-purpose flour

1 1/2 teaspoons ground cinnamon

1 teaspoon baking soda

1/2 teaspoon salt

1 cup sugar

3/4 cup vegetable oil

1/4 cup honey

1 egg

1 cup chopped pecans

CONFECTIONERS' SUGAR ICING

1 cup sifted confectioners' sugar

2 tablespoons margarine, melted

1 tablespoon water

1 tablespoon milk

method

BARS

Sift the flour, cinnamon, baking soda and salt together. Combine the sugar, oil and honey in a bowl and mix well. Add the egg and mix until blended. Stir in the flour mixture and pecans; the batter will be stiff. Pat the honey mixture into a lightly greased 9×13-inch baking pan or 10×15-inch baking pan and bake at 350 degrees for 20 minutes. Cool in the pan on a wire rack for 5 minutes.

ICING

Mix the confectioners' sugar, margarine, water and milk in a bowl until of a spreading consistency and spread over the warm baked layer. Let stand until set and cut into bars.

NOTE: *Honey that has crystallized is not spoiled. It can easily be reconstituted by placing the opened jar in a bowl of warm water or microwaving it for a few seconds. Be careful not to bring the honey to a boil, as that will damage both the quality and the flavor.*

TURTLE CANDY

Makes a variable amount

ingredients

1 bag pretzel squares

2 (11-ounce) bags Rolos candies

1 1/2 to 2 cups pecan halves

method

Arrange the pretzels in a single layer on a baking sheet. Top each pretzel with a candy. Bake at 250 degrees for 4 minutes. Press one pecan half into each candy. Chill in the refrigerator until ready to serve.

PEACH PIE BARS

· ·

Makes 2 to 3 dozen bars

ingredients

CRUST

3 cups all-purpose flour
3/4 cup packed brown sugar
1/4 teaspoon ground cinnamon
1/8 teaspoon salt
1 cup (2 sticks) unsalted butter,
    chilled and cut into 1-inch pieces

PEACH FILLING

2 cups peach jam or jelly
6 large peaches, each peeled and
    cut into 8 wedges

PECAN TOPPING

2 cups pecans
2 cups all-purpose flour
1 cup packed brown sugar
1 cup (2 sticks) unsalted butter,
    chilled and cut into 1-inch pieces

method

CRUST

Coat a 9×13-inch baking pan with butter or nonstick cooking spray. Mix the flour, brown sugar, cinnamon and salt in a food processor fitted with a metal blade. Add the butter and pulse until the butter is evenly incorporated and the mixture adheres. Press the dough over the bottom of the prepared pan and bake at 350 degrees for 18 to 20 minutes or until light brown. Cool on a wire rack for 15 to 20 minutes. Maintain the oven temperature.

FILLING

Spread the jam evenly over the baked layer. Arrange the peaches overlapping over the jam.

TOPPING

Spread the pecans in a single layer on a baking sheet. Toast for 7 to 9 minutes or until light brown and fragrant. Let stand until cool and chop. Maintain the oven temperature.

Combine the flour and brown sugar in a food processor fitted with a metal blade. Add the butter and pulse until crumbly. Stir in the pecans. Sprinkle the mixture over the top of the layers. Bake for 50 to 60 minutes or until the topping is golden brown. Cool in the pan on a wire rack and cut into bars.

To easily peel fresh peaches, cut an X in the bottom of each peach. Drop the peaches into a saucepan of boiling water for thirty seconds, and then plunge them into a bowl of cold water. The skins should slip off easily.

JULY

July is all about food, fun, and fireworks!

In fact, with so many spectacular Fourth of

riverblast

July celebrations to choose from in Northwest

celebration on the cane

Louisiana, you'll have no problem finding a place

northwestern folk festival

to let your patriotism shine. God bless America!

hodges gardens independence day festival

The summer sun begins to broil the Northwest Louisiana landscape in July, but that doesn't stop the fun. This month is almost synonymous with INDEPENDENCE DAY in this great country of ours, and food, family, and fireworks generally dominate the themes for local celebrations.

Since the mid-1800s, parades, picnics, and fireworks have been common traditions used to honor our country's fight for freedom. In keeping with tradition, Shreveport hosts the annual RIVERBLAST FESTIVAL, celebrating Independence Day with live entertainment, a children's area, and a truly spectacular fireworks display over the Red River.

You can find similar patriotic displays across the region, including the CELEBRATION ON THE CANE in Natchitoches, the oldest permanent settlement in the Louisiana Purchase territory. This old-fashioned Fourth of July celebration is complete with patriotic music and fireworks over the scenic Cane River Lake. THE HODGES GARDENS INDEPENDENCE DAY FESTIVAL, on the grounds of the nation's largest privately owned horticultural parkland and wildlife refuge near Many, Louisiana, also offers an annual event held on July 4th with fireworks, food, arts and crafts, and more.

If the July heat is just too much for you, the annual NATCHITOCHES/NORTHWESTERN FOLK FESTIVAL celebrates Louisiana's culture and folk life in the air-conditioned Prather Coliseum on the NSU campus. This event began in 1979 and is host to more than sixty master folk artists, craftsmen, and exhibitors. Listen to the sounds of Cajun, Zydeco, country, and folk musicians while you browse. Let your taste buds get in on the party, too, and choose from dozens of different Louisiana foods.

July is also peak season for summer fun on one of our many lakes. It's hard to find a more perfect backdrop for your Fourth of July picnic than Cross Lake. The Shreveport Yacht Club is found here, one of the few bodies of water in the state where sailing is offered. At Toledo Bend Reservoir, you'll find more than one state park and several lodging and camping facilities around this nationally renowned fishing lake. Scuba diving is also very popular near the dam area of the lake. Caddo Lake, sitting astride the Texas-Louisiana border, is considered by many to be the most unique and scenic lake in the state, with abundant fishing, a wildlife habitat, open areas for water sports, and acres of untouched cypress forest smothered in hanging Spanish moss. Lake Bistineau in Bossier Parish is one of the most picturesque areas in the state, where photographers come from near and far to capture the mystic beauty of the Louisiana swampland. And don't forget Cypress-Black Bayou, a family-friendly lake that is home to camping and lodging facilities, beaches for swimming, a nature center, and a petting zoo for the kids.

Inside or outside, day or night, there's no mistaking that Northwest Louisiana offers something for all. Join us in celebration of our nation . . . our state . . . our backyard.

JULY

RASPBERRY LEMONADE COOLERS

Serves 8

ingredients

12 ounces fresh raspberries

3 cups citron vodka

4 lemons, each cut into 8 slices

3 tablespoons sugar

6 cups lemonade (made from concentrate)

8 sprigs of mint

method

Mash the raspberries in a large bowl and mix in the vodka. Chill, covered, for 8 to 10 hours. Strain, pressing on the raspberries to extract additional juice; discard the solids. The raspberry vodka should measure about 3 cups.

Place the lemon wedges and sugar in a large pitcher and mash the lemons with a wooden spoon to release the juice. Add the raspberry vodka and lemonade and mix well. Chill, covered, in the refrigerator for up to 8 hours. Pour the lemonade and mashed lemons over ice in eight glasses. Garnish each serving with a mint sprig.

WATERMELON SLUSHY

Serves 4 to 6

ingredients

5 cups (1/2-inch) cubes seeded watermelon

1 cup orange juice, chilled

1 (6-ounce) can frozen limeade or lemonade concentrate

method

Arrange the watermelon in a single layer on a baking sheet and freeze for 45 to 60 minutes or until partially frozen. Process the watermelon, orange juice and limeade concentrate in a blender until smooth. Spoon the slush mixture into cups and serve with a straw, or freeze for future use.

FARMER'S MARKET SQUARES

Serves 10 to 12

ingredients

2 (8-count) cans crescent rolls
16 ounces cream cheese, softened
1 envelope ranch salad
    dressing mix
1 cup (4 ounces) shredded
    Cheddar cheese
1 cup chopped broccoli
1 cup chopped cauliflower
1 cup chopped black olives
1 cup chopped seeded tomato
1 cup grated carrots
1/2 cup chopped green onions

method

Unroll the crescent roll dough and pat into a rectangle on a baking sheet, sealing the edges and perforations. Bake at 375 degrees for 13 to 15 minutes or until light brown. Let stand until cool.

Beat the cream cheese and salad dressing mix in a mixing bowl until light and fluffy and spread over the baked layer. Toss the cheese, broccoli, cauliflower, olives, tomato, carrots and green onions in a bowl and sprinkle over the cream cheese. Cut into 1- to 2-inch squares.

STRAWBERRY MANGO SALSA*

Serves 8 to 10

ingredients

1 1/2 cups chopped fresh
    strawberries
1/2 cup chopped mango
1/2 cup chopped red bell pepper
1/3 cup chopped red onion
1/4 cup coarsely chopped cilantro
2 tablespoons lime juice
1 tablespoon sugar
2 teaspoons tequila (optional)
1/2 teaspoon salt

*Photograph for this recipe on page 111.

method

Combine the strawberries, mango, bell pepper, onion, cilantro, lime juice, sugar, tequila and salt in a bowl and mix gently. Chill, covered, for up to 8 hours.

PINEAPPLE MANGO SALSA*

- -

Serves 10 to 12

ingredients

2 mangoes, peeled and
    finely chopped
3 cups finely chopped fresh
    pineapple
1 cup chopped celery
1 (4-ounce) can chopped
    green chiles
1/2 cup chopped red onion
1/4 cup chopped red bell pepper
1/4 cup chopped fresh cilantro
1/4 cup lime juice

*Photograph for this recipe on page 111.

method

Combine the mangoes, pineapple, celery, green chiles, onion, bell pepper, cilantro and lime juice in a bowl and mix gently. Serve as a dip with tortilla scoops, or as an accompaniment to any grilled white fish.

You may substitute 1 large can of pineapple tidbits, drained and coarsely chopped, for the fresh pineapple.

HERBED TOMATOES*

- -

This is a great way to use the summer's bounty of homegrown tomatoes and herbs.
Serves 12

ingredients

6 large tomatoes, sliced
1 tablespoon chopped fresh thyme,
    or 1 teaspoon dried thyme
1 tablespoon chopped fresh
    marjoram, or 1 teaspoon
    dried marjoram
1/4 cup finely chopped fresh parsley
1/4 cup chopped fresh chives or
    green onion tops
1/2 teaspoon salt
1/4 teaspoon coarsely ground pepper
1/3 cup vegetable oil
1/4 cup tarragon vinegar

*Photograph for this recipe on page 111.

method

Layer the tomato slices in a deep bowl, sprinkling each layer with thyme, marjoram, parsley, chives, salt and pepper. Whisk the oil and vinegar in a bowl and pour over the layers. Chill, covered, until serving time. Drain the tomatoes, if desired, and serve the marinade with the tomatoes. Serve on sandwiches, on burgers or as a side dish. Chop the tomatoes, spread on crostini and sprinkle with cheese for a simple appetizer.

FRUITY SPRING SALAD MIX

Serves 8

SWEET HOT VINAIGRETTE
1/4 cup vegetable oil
1/4 cup balsamic vinegar
2 tablespoons sugar
1/4 teaspoon salt
1/4 teaspoon pepper
1/4 teaspoon hot sauce

SUGARED ALMONDS
1 cup slivered almonds
1/2 cup sugar

SALAD
4 kiwifruit, peeled
2 (10-ounce) packages gourmet
    mixed salad greens
2 cups chopped fresh pineapple
1 (11-ounce) can mandarin
    oranges, drained
1 cup green grapes, cut lengthwise
    into halves
1 cup red grapes, cut lengthwise
    into halves

method

VINAIGRETTE
Combine the oil, vinegar, sugar, salt, pepper and hot sauce in a jar with a tight-fitting lid and seal tightly. Shake to combine. Chill for 30 minutes.

ALMONDS
Combine the almonds and sugar in a heavy saucepan and mix well. Cook over medium heat until golden brown, stirring constantly. Spread the almond mixture in a single layer on a sheet of lightly greased waxed paper and let cool for 20 minutes. Break into bite-size pieces.

SALAD
Slice the kiwifruit and cut the slices into halves. Toss the kiwifruit, salad greens, pineapple, mandarin oranges and grapes in a large salad bowl. Drizzle with the vinaigrette and sprinkle with the almonds. Serve immediately.

*I*nstead of using ice, freeze water in clean plastic milk jugs and place them in coolers to keep everything cold. The cooler will not fill up with water from the melted ice, and you will have cold drinking water available during the picnic or tailgate party.

ORIENTAL ASPARAGUS SALAD

Serves 4

ingredients

1 pound asparagus, trimmed and
    cut into 2-inch pieces
2 tablespoons soy sauce
1 tablespoon vegetable oil
1 tablespoon rice wine vinegar
1 1/2 teaspoons sugar
1 teaspoon sesame seeds, toasted
1/4 to 1/2 teaspoon ground ginger
1/4 teaspoon ground cumin

method

Cook the asparagus in a small amount of water in a saucepan for 3 to 4 minutes or until tender-crisp and drain. Place the asparagus in a large bowl.

Whisk the soy sauce, oil, vinegar, sugar, sesame seeds, ginger and cumin in a bowl until combined and pour over the asparagus, tossing to coat. Chill, covered, for 1 hour. Drain before serving.

EASY COLESLAW*

Serves 8

ingredients

1/4 cup white vinegar
2 tablespoons low-fat mayonnaise
1 tablespoon Dijon mustard
1 1/2 teaspoons sugar
Salt and freshly ground pepper
    to taste
2 cups shredded cabbage
1/2 cup sliced carrots
1/2 cup sliced sweet or purple onion

*Photograph for this recipe on page 111.

method

Mix the vinegar, mayonnaise, Dijon mustard, sugar, salt and pepper in a bowl. Add the cabbage, carrots and onion and mix until coated. Taste and adjust the seasonings, adding additional Dijon mustard, salt and/or pepper as needed.

K.C. BAKED BEANS*

. . . .

Serves 6 to 8

ingredients

4 (15-ounce) cans pork and
  beans, drained
2 Granny Smith apples, peeled
  and chopped
2 onions, chopped
1½ cups barbecue sauce
1 cup packed brown sugar

*Photograph for this recipe on page 111.

method

Combine the pork and beans, apples, onions, barbecue sauce and brown sugar in a bowl and mix well. Spoon the bean mixture into a greased 9×13-inch baking dish and bake at 350 degrees for 1 hour.

SWEET 'N' HOT GREEN BEANS AND CARROTS*

. . . .

You can store this in a jar and eat them like pickles.

Serves 4 to 6

ingredients

½ cup sugar
½ cup white wine vinegar
¼ to ½ teaspoon crushed red
  pepper flakes
1 garlic clove, minced
8 ounces fresh green beans,
  trimmed
8 ounces carrots, cut into
  ½×4-inch strips

*Photograph for this recipe on page 111.

method

Whisk the sugar and vinegar in a bowl until the sugar dissolves. Stir in the red pepper flakes and garlic. Let stand, covered, at room temperature for 4 hours.

Cook the green beans and carrots in boiling water in a saucepan for 1 minute and drain. Immediately plunge the vegetables into a bowl of ice water to stop the cooking process and drain again. Pour the vinegar mixture over the vegetables in a bowl and toss to coat. Let stand at room temperature for 1 hour before serving.

ROASTED CORN ON THE COB

Serves 6

ingredients

6 fresh ears yellow corn with husks
1/4 cup (1/2 stick) butter
1 teaspoon basil
1 teaspoon Pickapeppa Sauce
1/2 teaspoon Creole seasoning
1/4 teaspoon pepper

method

Pull the corn husks back, leaving the husks attached at the base of the cob. Remove the silk. Rinse the corn and pat dry with paper towels.

Melt the butter in a small saucepan over low heat. Stir in the basil, Pickapeppa Sauce, Creole seasoning and pepper. Brush the corn with the butter mixture and reposition the husks. Arrange the corn on the grill rack. Grill, covered with the lid, over high heat (400 to 500 degrees) for 25 minutes, making quarter turns every 6 to 7 minutes. Pull the husks down and tie at the base of the cob to form a handle and serve immediately.

STRAWN'S EAT SHOP FRIED CHICKEN*

Serves 6

ingredients

1 cup salt
6 chicken breasts
1 cup Accent
1 cup Lawry's seasoning
1 tablespoon red pepper
1 1/2 teaspoons garlic powder
4 cups (or more) all-purpose flour
1/4 to 1/2 cup vegetable oil

*Photograph for this recipe on page 111.

method

Combine the salt with enough cold water to cover the chicken in a large container and stir until the salt dissolves. Add the chicken and marinate in the refrigerator for 8 to 10 hours. Drain and pat dry.

Mix the Accent, Lawry's seasoning, red pepper and garlic powder in a shallow dish and stir in the flour. Taste for spiciness and saltiness and add additional flour if too spicy or salty. Coat the chicken breasts one at a time in the flour mixture. Heat the oil in a deep skillet over high heat. Add the chicken to the hot oil and fry until cooked through and golden brown. Drain and serve immediately.

STEAK TERIYAKI

Serves 6

ingredients

1/2 cup soy sauce
1/4 cup sherry
2 tablespoons honey
2 tablespoons white wine vinegar
1 tablespoon minced fresh ginger
1 1/2 pounds flank steak, sliced
1/4 cup vegetable oil

method

Whisk the soy sauce, sherry, honey, vinegar and ginger in a bowl until combined. Pour the soy sauce mixture over the steak in a shallow dish, turning to coat. Marinate, covered, in the refrigerator for 4 hours or longer, turning occasionally; drain.

Heat the oil in a skillet and add the steak. Fry until light brown on both sides, turning occasionally. Thread the steak on large bamboo skewers, if desired, and grill over hot coals.

BEEF BRISKET*

Serves 8 to 12

ingredients

1 (4- to 6-pound) beef brisket
Chopped onion
2 (3-ounce) bottles liquid smoke
1/2 bottle Worcestershire sauce
Salt and pepper to taste
1 bottle barbecue sauce

*Photograph for this recipe on page 111.

method

Place the brisket in a large sealable plastic bag or in a shallow dish and cover with onion. Pour the liquid smoke over the top and seal tightly or cover. Marinate in the refrigerator for 8 to 10 hours.

Drain the brisket and place on a sheet of heavy-duty foil large enough to cover the brisket. Drizzle with the Worcestershire sauce and sprinkle with salt and pepper. Seal tightly. Place the foil-covered brisket in a baking pan and bake at 275 degrees for 6 hours. Open the foil and pour the barbecue sauce over the top. Bake for 1 hour longer. Slice or shred as desired.

FRUIT PIZZA*

• •

Serves 15

*Photograph for this recipe on page 111.

ingredients

1 roll refrigerator sugar
   cookie dough
8 ounces cream cheese, softened
1/4 cup sugar
1 tablespoon vanilla extract
Sliced kiwifruit
Sliced fresh strawberries
Sliced bananas
Fresh blueberries
Strawberry glaze

method

Pat the cookie dough over the bottom of a 9×13-inch baking pan or a pizza pan. Bake at 375 degrees for 10 minutes. Do not allow to brown. Let stand until cool.

Beat the cream cheese, sugar and vanilla in a mixing bowl until creamy. Spread the cream cheese mixture evenly over the baked layer. Top with kiwifruit, strawberries, bananas and blueberries and drizzle with strawberry glaze. Chill, covered, until serving time. You may substitute apple jelly for the strawberry glaze. Melt the jelly before drizzling over the layers.

WHITE CHOCOLATE RASPBERRY TART

• •

Cut into bite-size pieces for an elegant cocktail buffet dessert.
Serves 8

ingredients

12 ounces white chocolate
1/2 cup heavy cream, heated
1/4 cup (1/2 stick) unsalted
   butter, softened
2 cups fresh raspberries
1 baked graham cracker or pecan
   shortbread pie shell
Raspberries

method

Melt the chocolate in a double boiler over simmering water until smooth, stirring occasionally. Stir in the warm cream and butter. Remove from the heat.

Arrange 2 cups raspberries evenly over the bottom of the pie shell and pour the chocolate mixture over the raspberries. Chill for 1 hour or until firm. Garnish with additional raspberries.

FOURTH OF JULY TRIFLE*

Serves 10 to 12

ingredients

2 quarts fresh strawberries, sliced
Granulated sugar to taste
16 ounces cream cheese, softened
2 cups confectioners' sugar
1 cup sour cream
2 teaspoons vanilla extract
1/4 teaspoon almond extract
1 cup whipping cream
1 tablespoon granulated sugar
1 teaspoon vanilla extract
1 (10-inch) angel food cake, cubed
2 pints blueberries
4 bananas, sliced

*Photograph for this recipe on page 111.

method

Sprinkle the strawberries with granulated sugar to taste in a bowl and set aside. Beat the cream cheese and confectioners' sugar in a large mixing bowl until creamy. Add the sour cream, 2 teaspoons vanilla and the almond extract and beat until smooth. Beat the whipping cream in a mixing bowl until soft peaks form. Add 1 tablespoon granulated sugar and 1 teaspoon vanilla and beat until firm peaks form.

Fold the whipped cream into the cream cheese mixture. Add the cake cubes and mix gently. Layer the blueberries and one-half of the cake mixture in a trifle bowl. Top with the bananas, remaining cake mixture and undrained strawberries in the order listed. Chill, covered, until serving time. You may assemble and serve this in individual dessert bowls.

BANANA SPLIT CAKE

Serves 15

ingredients

2 cups graham cracker crumbs
1/2 cup (1 stick) butter, melted
1/4 cup granulated sugar
1 (1-pound) package
   confectioners' sugar
1/2 cup (1 stick) butter, softened
2 egg whites
3 or 4 bananas, sliced
1 (20-ounce) can crushed
   pineapple, drained
16 ounces whipped topping
1 cup chopped pecans
1 jar maraschino cherries, drained

method

Mix the graham cracker crumbs, 1/2 cup melted butter and the granulated sugar in a bowl. Press the crumb mixture over the bottom of a 9×13-inch cake pan.

Beat the confectioners' sugar, 1/2 cup softened butter and the egg whites in a mixing bowl for 15 minutes, scraping the bowl occasionally. Spread over the prepared crust. Layer with the bananas, pineapple and whipped topping in the order listed. Sprinkle with the pecans and maraschino cherries.

JACK DANIEL'S ICE CREAM SAUCE

Makes 3 cups

ingredients

2 cups light corn syrup
1½ cups packed light brown sugar
¼ cup (½ stick) butter
⅛ teaspoon salt, or to taste
¾ cup Jack Daniel's whiskey

method

Combine the corn syrup, brown sugar, butter and salt in a saucepan and cook over low heat until the brown sugar dissolves, stirring frequently. Increase the heat and bring to a slow boil. Stir in the whiskey. Serve warm over ice cream.

The air-conditioned comfort of the Sci-Port Discovery Center on the downtown Shreveport riverfront promises a hands-on educational and entertaining environment for people of all ages and is a great place to beat the heat. For a truly awesome experience, take in a show at the center's sixty-foot IMAX® Dome Theater. This spectacular theater, which is open to the public 362 days a year, is the only one of its kind in Louisiana and one of only twenty-eight in the entire nation.

AUGUST

james burton international guitar festival

annual gentleman's cooking classic

weekends live in the red river district

river cities triathlon

Although August is the hottest month of the year, it doesn't stifle the fun. Escape the heat in the cool waters of the Red River or an area lake, or take the party indoors at the Red River District, the Louisiana Boardwalk, or one of several riverboat casinos.

By the time August rolls around, temperatures have reached their hottest for the year. Summer's end is in sight, and local students know school is rapidly approaching. While there are fewer festivals this month as Northwest Louisiana tries to keep cool, August brings many opportunities for fun and celebration.

THE JAMES BURTON INTERNATIONAL GUITAR FESTIVAL in Shreveport is a three-day extravaganza that is sure to keep you rockin' while you enjoy good food and a tribute to James Burton, Shreveport's own Rock and Roll Hall of Fame inductee. He got his start at age fourteen playing for the Louisiana Hayride in the mid-1950s. During his career he performed as lead guitarist for Ricky Nelson, Elvis Presley, John Denver, and Jerry Lee Lewis. He also played on records for the Beach Boys, Merle Haggard, and Sonny and Cher. He is still active in the industry, and we're proud he calls Northwest Louisiana home.

In Shreveport, WEEKENDS LIVE IN THE RED RIVER DISTRICT features the very best in local and regional musical acts performing on the Downtown River District's center stage. There is also the ANNUAL GENTLEMAN'S COOKING CLASSIC held at the Expo Hall, which features local celebrity chefs and restaurants cooking everything from their own favorite recipes to family recipes handed down for generations.

If you have energy to spare, come to Cypress Black Bayou for a celebration of a different kind. Celebrate fitness and dedication as you cheer on local, regional, and national athletes who conclude months of hard work and preparation at the RIVER CITIES TRIATHLON. This athletic event, which includes swimming, biking, and running all in one race, is the oldest, largest, and most recognized triathlon in the South. It has been a proud Shreveport-Bossier City tradition since 1980. Whether you are a racer or a spectator, you'll appreciate the upbeat, healthy, and festive atmosphere, complete with food, music, and camaraderie after the race. Be careful though, you just may catch triathlon fever!

Before the summer ends, be sure to take advantage of one of the area's greatest natural resources. Navigation and commerce on the Red River were the reasons the sister cities of Shreveport and Bossier City were founded more than a century and a half ago. Today, you can enjoy one of the benefits of its recent revival and spend time together with family and friends on the Red River. With open water stretching unimpeded for miles, you're sure to run out of energy before you run out of ways to have fun.

When the shadows grow longer, no matter which side of the neon-lit Texas Street Bridge the evening finds you on, excitement awaits in the Red River District in Shreveport and at the Louisiana Boardwalk in Bossier City. There you'll find enough great food, shopping, and live entertainment to continue the fun well into the night. Or, if you're feeling lucky, bet on one of the riverboat casinos in the area for gambling, big-name concerts, and restaurants to satisfy almost any appetite.

Whether you're into rockin' or racing, cooking or casinos, August has got you covered!

ELECTRIC LEMONADE

● ●

Serves 8

ingredients

2 cups sugar

2 cups water

1 cup fresh lemon juice

1 cup (8 ounces) lemon-flavored
   vodka

method

Combine the sugar and 2 cups water in a saucepan. Cook over medium heat until the sugar is dissolved and the mixture is of a syrup consistency, stirring constantly. Stir in the lemon juice. Pour into ice cube trays and freeze. Combine the ice cubes, vodka and a splash of water in a blender and process until slushy.

ALMOND TEA

● ●

Serve in a punch bowl or over ice in glasses.
Makes 1 gallon

ingredients

3 lemons, cut into halves

1 quart water

2 cups sugar

2 cups brewed tea
   (6 family-size tea bags)

2½ cups pineapple juice

2 teaspoons vanilla extract

2 teaspoons almond extract

1 quart ginger ale

method

Squeeze the lemon halves to extract the juice, reserving the juice and lemon shells. Combine the reserved lemon shells, water and sugar in a saucepan and bring to a boil. Boil for 3 minutes and discard the lemon shells. Stir in the reserved lemon juice, tea, pineapple juice and flavorings. Pour the tea mixture into a covered container and chill until serving time. Add the ginger ale just before serving.

LOUISIANA CRAB CAKES WITH SAUCE RAVIGOTTE

This recipe comes from Fertitta's Bistro 6301, a family-owned restaurant that has enjoyed
local success in the Arkansas, Louisiana, and Texas area for more than thirty years.
Makes 6 to 8 crab cakes

ingredients

SAUCE RAVIGOTTE
1¹/2 cups mayonnaise
¹/8 teaspoon white pepper
Worcestershire sauce to taste
Tabasco sauce to taste
¹/2 cup chopped drained capers
¹/2 cup chopped drained dill pickles
¹/4 cup chopped fresh parsley

CRAB CAKES
¹/4 cup Creole mustard, such as
   Zatarain's
¹/4 cup mayonnaise
3 eggs, lightly beaten
Cayenne pepper to taste
1 pound Louisiana lump
   crab meat, drained, shells and
   cartilage removed
¹/4 cup finely chopped green onions
¹/4 cup bread crumbs or
   cracker crumbs
1 cup milk
2 eggs
1¹/2 cups all-purpose flour
Tony Chachere's seasoning to taste
Olive oil

method

SAUCE
Combine the mayonnaise, white pepper, Worcestershire sauce and Tabasco sauce in a bowl and mix well. Stir in the capers, dill pickles and parsley. Chill, covered, in the refrigerator.

CRAB CAKES
Mix the Creole mustard, mayonnaise and 3 eggs in a bowl and season with cayenne pepper. Fold in the crab meat; do not break up the lumps. Gently stir in the green onions and bread crumbs; the mixture should be moist. Shape the crab meat mixture into cakes, 3 inches in diameter and ³/4 inch thick. Arrange the patties on a baking sheet lined with waxed paper and chill until firm.

Whisk the milk and 2 eggs in a bowl until blended. Mix the flour and Tony Chachere's seasoning in a bowl. Dip each crab cake in the egg mixture and coat lightly with the flour mixture. Heat enough olive oil in a skillet to measure ¹/4 inch and add the crab cakes. Fry until golden brown and drain. Serve with the sauce.

*S*hreveport's Louisiana Hayride debuted in 1948 in the Municipal Auditorium. It was the stage for Elvis Presley's first national broadcast. It also ignited the careers of Hank Williams, Sr., Slim Whitman, and Johnny Cash.

MINIATURE TOMATO SANDWICHES

· ·

Makes 16 sandwiches

ingredients

1/4 cup mayonnaise

3 ounces cream cheese, softened

2 teaspoons chopped fresh basil

1/4 teaspoon salt

1/4 teaspoon pepper

1 baguette

4 plum tomatoes, sliced and drained

method

Combine the mayonnaise, cream cheese, basil, 1/8 teaspoon salt and 1/8 teaspoon pepper in a bowl and mix well. Chill, covered, for 8 hours.

Cut the baguette into sixteen slices. Spread the cream cheese mixture on one side of each slice and top each with one or two tomato slices. Sprinkle with the remaining 1/8 teaspoon salt and 1/8 teaspoon pepper and serve immediately.

*W*hen adding tomatoes to your sandwiches, first salt them on both sides. Drain them on a rack or in a colander for fifteen minutes and pat dry with paper towels. This will prevent soggy sandwiches.

FRUIT SALSA WITH CINNAMON-SUGAR CRISPS

Makes 2 cups salsa

ingredients

SALSA

1 quart fresh strawberries,
   finely chopped
1 Red Delicious apple,
   finely chopped
6 kiwifruit, peeled and
   finely chopped
3 bananas, finely chopped
1/2 cup fresh lemon juice
1/2 cup sugar

CINNAMON-SUGAR CRISPS

2 tablespoons sugar
1 tablespoon ground cinnamon
1 (12-count) package flour tortillas
   for soft tacos

method

SALSA

Combine the strawberries, apple, kiwifruit, bananas, lemon juice and sugar in a bowl and mix gently. Chill, covered, for 2 hours.

CRISPS

Mix the sugar and cinnamon in a bowl. Coat the tortillas one at a time with butter-flavor nonstick cooking spray and sprinkle each with the sugar mixture. Cut into strips and arrange on a baking sheet coated with nonstick cooking spray. Bake at 375 degrees for 8 to 10 minutes or until light brown and crisp. Remove to a wire rack to cool. Serve with the salsa. Store leftovers in an airtight container.

*C*innamon is the highly aromatic bark from a small evergreen tree. It is one of the oldest-known spices and is the one most widely used in baking.

ARTICHOKE BREAD

Makes 16 slices

ingredients

2 loaves French bread
1/2 cup (1 stick) butter
2 garlic cloves, minced
1 (14-ounce) can artichoke hearts,
    drained and chopped
2 cups sour cream
8 to 10 ounces mozzarella
    cheese, shredded
8 to 10 ounces Cheddar
    cheese, shredded
Cayenne pepper to taste
Paprika to taste
Grated Parmesan cheese to taste

method

Cut a thin slice from the top of each bread loaf. Remove the center of each loaf carefully, leaving a 1-inch shell. Cut the bread from the center into cubes.

Melt the butter in a skillet. Sauté the garlic in the butter and stir in the reserved bread cubes, artichokes and sour cream. Stir in one-half of the mozzarella cheese and one-half of the Cheddar cheese. Season with cayenne pepper and paprika.

Spoon the artichoke mixture evenly into the bread shells and sprinkle with the remaining mozzarella cheese, remaining Cheddar cheese, the Parmesan cheese and additional paprika. Bake at 350 degrees for 15 to 20 minutes. Cut each loaf into 8 slices.

EASY CHEDDAR BISCUITS

Makes 1 1/2 dozen biscuits

ingredients

1 1/2 cups all-purpose flour
1 tablespoon baking powder
1 tablespoon sugar
1/2 teaspoon salt
1 cup (4 ounces) shredded sharp
    Cheddar cheese
1/3 cup shortening
1/2 cup milk

method

Combine the flour, baking powder, sugar and salt in a food processor and pulse 4 or 5 times until combined. Add the cheese and shortening and pulse 4 or 5 times until crumbly. Add the milk gradually, processing constantly until the dough forms a ball and pulls from the side of the bowl.

Shape the dough into a ball on a lightly floured surface. Pat or roll 1/2 inch thick and cut with a biscuit cutter into rounds. Arrange the rounds on a baking sheet and bake at 425 degrees for 10 minutes or until golden brown. Serve warm.

YOGURT AND CUCUMBER SALAD

Serves 2

ingredients

1 garlic clove
1/2 teaspoon salt
1 cup plain yogurt
1/2 teaspoon mint
1 cucumber, peeled and chopped

method

Mash the garlic and salt in a bowl. Stir in the yogurt and mint and fold in the cucumber. Chill, covered, to allow the flavors to marry. Serve alone or with pita bread.

VEGETABLE COUSCOUS SALAD

Serves 8

ingredients

BALSAMIC ITALIAN DRESSING
1/3 cup water
1/4 cup balsamic vinegar
1 tablespoon olive oil
1 envelope Italian salad
   dressing mix

SALAD
1 1/2 cups water
1 cup couscous
2 cups chopped red bell pepper
2 cups chopped tomatoes
1/2 cup crumbled feta cheese
1/2 cup finely chopped green onions
1/4 cup chopped kalamata olives
1/4 cup chopped fresh parsley

method

DRESSING

Combine the water, vinegar, olive oil and salad dressing mix in a jar with a tight-fitting lid and seal tightly. Shake to mix.

SALAD

Bring the water to a boil in a saucepan and add the couscous gradually, stirring constantly. Remove from the heat and let stand, covered, for 5 minutes. Fluff with a fork. Combine the couscous, bell pepper, tomatoes, cheese, green onions, olives and parsley in a large bowl and mix well. Add the dressing and toss gently until coated.

PASTA SALAD WITH STEAK

Serves 4

ingredients

PASTA

3/4 cup olive oil

2 tablespoons lemon juice

1 tablespoon Dijon mustard

2 teaspoons oregano

2 teaspoons red wine vinegar

1 teaspoon sugar

1/2 teaspoon salt

1/2 teaspoon pepper

3 cups cooked small shell pasta

STEAK

1 (1-pound) sirloin steak

1 tablespoon olive oil

3 garlic cloves, minced

2 teaspoons oregano

2 teaspoons pepper

1 teaspoon sugar

SALAD

2/3 cup chopped cucumber

1/3 cup crumbled feta cheese

1/4 cup sliced black olives

1/4 cup chopped red onion

1/4 cup chopped fresh parsley

1 (2-ounce) jar pimento, drained

Iceberg lettuce or romaine

method

PASTA

Combine the olive oil, lemon juice, Dijon mustard, oregano, vinegar, sugar, salt and pepper in a jar with a tight-fitting lid and seal tightly. Shake to mix. Reserve one-half of the dressing. Pour the remaining dressing over the pasta in a bowl and toss to coat. Chill, covered, in the refrigerator.

STEAK

Pierce the steak with a fork. Mix the olive oil, garlic, oregano, pepper and sugar in a bowl and rub over the surface of the steak. Chill, covered, for 15 minutes or longer. Grill the steak over medium heat for 9 to 10 minutes on each side or until a meat thermometer registers 140 degrees for rare, 160 degrees for medium or 170 degrees for well-done. Let stand for 10 minutes and cut into strips.

SALAD

Add the cucumber, cheese, olives, onion, parsley and pimento to the chilled pasta and mix well. Line four serving plates with lettuce and spoon one-fourth of the pasta salad on each plate. Top evenly with the steak and serve with the reserved dressing.

CORN WITH ZUCCHINI AND PEPPER JACK CHEESE

Serves 4

ingredients

4 fresh ears of corn with husks
2 tablespoons olive oil
1 zucchini, cut into $1/3$-inch pieces
Salt to taste
1 cup finely chopped red onion
1 cup (4 ounces) coarsely shredded
   Pepper Jack cheese
2 tablespoons finely crushed
   tortilla chips

method

Pull a lengthwise 1- to $1^{1}/_{2}$-inch strip of husk from each ear of corn to expose a strip of kernels. Discard the husk strip. Carefully peel back the remaining husks, keeping them attached at the stem end. Snap the ears from the stem ends and discard the silk.

Tear a thin strip from a tender inner piece of each husk and use it to tie the loose ends of each husk, forming a boat. Cut the kernels from the ears and discard the cobs.

Heat the olive oil in a large skillet and add the zucchini. Sauté for 2 minutes or until brown and tender. Remove to a bowl using a slotted spoon, reserving the pan drippings. Season the zucchini with salt. Sauté the corn kernels and onion in the reserved pan drippings over medium-high heat for 4 minutes. Cook, covered, for 2 to 3 minutes longer or until the corn is tender-crisp. Stir in the zucchini and season with salt. Let stand until cool and stir in the cheese.

Arrange the corn husk boats on a baking sheet and spoon the corn mixture evenly into the boats. Sprinkle with the crushed tortilla chips and place the baking sheet in the upper one-third of the oven. Bake at 375 degrees for 15 to 20 minutes or until bubbly.

CORN SOUFFLÉ

Serves 4 to 6

ingredients

1/2 cup (1 stick) butter
1/2 cup packed brown sugar
1 tablespoon all-purpose flour
1 1/2 teaspoons baking powder
1/2 (12-ounce) can evaporated milk
2 eggs, beaten
24 ounces frozen corn kernels
1/2 teaspoon cinnamon-sugar
Butter, sliced

method

Melt 1/2 cup butter in a medium saucepan and stir in the brown sugar. Add a mixture of the flour and baking powder and mix well. Stir in the evaporated milk. Remove from the heat and stir in the eggs. Add the corn and mix well.

Spoon the corn mixture into a buttered baking dish and sprinkle with the cinnamon-sugar. Dot with sliced butter and bake at 350 degrees for 30 minutes.

TORTA RUSTICA

Serves 6 to 8

ingredients

2 cans refrigerator pizza dough
1 pound bulk pork sausage
1/4 cup finely chopped fresh parsley
1/4 cup (1 ounce) grated
   Parmesan cheese
3 tomatoes, sliced
1 1/2 to 2 cups (6 to 8 ounces)
   shredded mozzarella cheese
1 egg, beaten

method

Roll 1 can of the dough on a lightly floured surface and fit into a 9×13-inch baking dish. Brown the sausage in a skillet, stirring until crumbly; drain. Combine the sausage, parsley and Parmesan cheese in a bowl and mix well. Spread the sausage mixture evenly over the prepared layer and top with the tomatoes and mozzarella cheese.

Roll the remaining can of dough on a lightly floured surface and cut into 1-inch strips. Arrange the strips lattice-fashion over the top. Brush with the egg and bake at 350 degrees for 35 minutes. Cool before slicing.

STRIP STEAK WITH TOMATOES AND OLIVES

Serves 2

ingredients

2 ripe plum tomatoes, seeded and
  cut into 1/4-inch pieces
1/4 cup plus 1 tablespoon coarsely
  chopped green olives
Coarse salt and freshly ground
  pepper to taste
1 tablespoon extra-virgin olive oil
1 tablespoon coarsely chopped
  fresh parsley
2 teaspoons balsamic vinegar
1 (1-pound) prime-aged New York
  strip steak, 1 1/2 inches thick
1 tablespoon coarsely chopped
  fresh parsley

method

Combine the tomatoes and olives in a small bowl and mix well. Season with salt and pepper and stir in the olive oil, 1 tablespoon parsley and the vinegar.

Arrange the steak on a rack in a broiler pan and broil 4 inches from the heat source for 4 minutes or until brown and turn. Broil for 3 minutes longer for medium-rare or 4 minutes longer for medium.

Let the steak rest for 5 minutes. Cut into 1/4-inch slices and arrange the slices on a serving platter. Spoon the tomato mixture over the steak and sprinkle with 1 tablespoon parsley. Serve immediately.

NOTE: *When choosing a steak, look for beef with good marbling (fat that runs throughout). This keeps the beef from shrinking and drying as it cooks.*

*I*s a rare steak really bloody? No! The blood in meat is drained at the slaughterhouse and hardly any ever remains. There is a pigment called myoglobin in all meat that contributes to the reddish color. Myoglobin is found in the muscles but not in the arteries or blood; therefore, those red juices are primarily colored by myoglobin.

APRICOT-GLAZED CHICKEN

Serves 4 to 6

ingredients

1½ cups apricot jam
2 tablespoons olive oil
1 tablespoon dry mustard
1 tablespoon sherry vinegar
Cayenne pepper to taste
4 to 6 chicken breasts
Salt and black pepper to taste

method

Combine the jam, olive oil, dry mustard, vinegar and cayenne pepper in a bowl and mix well. Season the chicken with salt and black pepper and brush with the jam mixture.

Arrange the chicken in a single layer in a baking pan and roast at 400 degrees for 10 minutes, basting with the jam mixture occasionally. Turn the chicken and roast for 10 minutes longer or until cooked through, basting with the jam mixture occasionally.

BAKED FISH WITH PARMESAN SOUR CREAM SAUCE

Serves 4 to 6

ingredients

1½ pounds tilapia fillets
1 cup light sour cream
¼ cup (1 ounce) shredded
    Parmesan cheese
½ teaspoon paprika
½ teaspoon salt
¼ teaspoon pepper
2 tablespoons Italian-style
    bread crumbs
2 tablespoons butter, melted

method

Arrange the fillets in a single layer in a lightly greased 9×13-inch baking dish. Combine the sour cream, cheese, paprika, salt and pepper in a bowl and mix well.

Spread the sour cream mixture evenly over the fillets and sprinkle with the bread crumbs. Drizzle with the butter and bake at 350 degrees for 20 to 25 minutes or until the fillets flake easily when tested with a fork.

LEMONADE CAKE

• •

Serves 16

ingredients

1 (2-layer) package lemon cake mix
3/4 cup water
3/4 cup canola oil
4 eggs, lightly beaten
1 (4-ounce) package lemon instant
    pudding mix
1 (6-ounce) can frozen lemonade
    concentrate, thawed
1/2 cup sugar

method

Combine the cake mix, water, canola oil, eggs and pudding mix in a bowl and mix well. Spoon the batter into a bundt pan sprayed with nonstick cooking spray. Bake at 350 degrees for 1 hour.

Combine the lemonade concentrate and sugar in a bowl and mix well. Pierce the top of the warm cake with a wooden pick and drizzle with the lemonade mixture. Cool in the pan on a wire rack for 1 hour to allow the mixture to be absorbed.

MANDARIN ORANGE CAKE

• •

Serves 12 to 16

ingredients

CAKE
1 (2-layer) package yellow cake mix
1 cup vegetable oil
1 (11-ounce) can mandarin oranges
    in heavy syrup
4 eggs

PINEAPPLE ICING
1 (20-ounce) can crushed
    pineapple, drained
1 (4-ounce) package vanilla instant
    pudding mix
16 ounces whipped topping

method

CAKE
Combine the cake mix, oil, undrained mandarin oranges and eggs in a mixing bowl and beat for 2 minutes, scraping the bowl occasionally. Spoon the batter into three greased and floured cake pans and bake at 350 degrees for 25 to 30 minutes or until the layers test done. Cool in the pans for 10 minutes and remove to a wire rack to cool completely.

ICING
Mix the pineapple and pudding mix in a bowl and fold in the whipped topping. Spread the icing between the layers and over the top and side of the cake. Store, covered, in the refrigerator.

STRAWBERRY DAIQUIRI PIES

This is a great summer dessert. Men love it.

Serves 12 to 16

ingredients

1 (14-ounce) can sweetened
 condensed milk
1 can frozen strawberry
 daiquiri concentrate
16 ounces whipped topping
2 (9-inch) graham cracker
 pie shells

method

Combine the condensed milk, daiquiri concentrate and whipped topping in a bowl and mix well. Spoon the whipped topping mixture evenly into the pie shells and freeze, covered, until firm. Serve frozen. You may store in the freezer for up to 1 week.

LEMONADE COOKIES

Makes 5 dozen cookies

ingredients

2 3/4 cups all-purpose flour
1 teaspoon baking soda
1 cup (2 sticks) butter, softened
3/4 cup sugar
1 1/4 cups sweetened lemonade mix
1 egg
1 teaspoon vanilla extract
1/2 teaspoon lemon extract, or
 1 teaspoon grated lemon zest

method

Mix the flour and baking soda together. Beat the butter, sugar and 3/4 cup of the lemonade mix in a mixing bowl until fluffy. Add the egg and flavorings and beat until blended. Beat in the flour mixture until a smooth dough forms.

Pour the remaining 1/2 cup lemonade mix into a shallow dish. Shape the dough into 1-inch balls and coat each ball with the lemonade mix. Arrange 2 inches apart on a greased cookie sheet and bake for 10 to 12 minutes or until brown around the edges. Cool on the cookie sheet for 2 minutes and remove to a wire rack to cool completely. Store in an airtight container.

SEPTEMBER

September brings the official end of summer,

the beginning of a new school year, and the

drake's salt works saline creek festival

celebration of Labor Day. It's also filled with

pioneer days

festivals to celebrate our region's rich heritage

super derby festival of racing

and fun-filled tailgating parties to get the

football season into full swing.

While the official end of summer isn't marked until later in September, we traditionally say goodbye on LABOR DAY, the first Monday of the month. Over the years, it has evolved from a celebration in honor of the working class into a "last fling of summer" holiday. And just as in any other part of the country, food and fun prevail in Northwest Louisiana.

Every year on the Saturday of Labor Day weekend, you can discover a savory little celebration at the DRAKE'S SALT WORKS SALINE CREEK FESTIVAL in Goldonna. The festival celebrates the history of Drake's Salt Works, where archeological artifacts span a period from 3000 B.C. to 1700 A.D. Drake's is also the site of what was, in 1830, the deepest drilled well in the world. During the Civil War, it was also a major source of salt for the Confederacy. Activities at the event include a parade, live entertainment, arts and crafts, food, family activities, and a Civil War reenactment, as well as fireworks at dark.

The arrival of more temperate fall weather makes September a perfect month to attend local events. See why Natchitoches has been called "the best little town in the whole USA" when you visit the CANE RIVER ZYDECO FESTIVAL. While enjoying the spirited Cajun music, you can also find authentic Louisiana cuisine, a poker run, and other fun and games. Or visit the PIONEER DAYS FESTIVAL in Greenwood, one of the few cities west of Shreveport before the Texas border. There you will find plenty of arts and crafts, concessions, games, entertainment, a parade, and contests in the town square.

It's no secret that sports are important to the people of Northwest Louisiana. After all, this is "Sportsman's Paradise." When it comes to team competition, Northwest Louisiana fans go wild over football. For the really die-hard fans, there's nothing like a day trip to the game for a rowdy tailgating party. The region offers several opportunities to experience LIVE COLLEGE FOOTBALL, such as at Louisiana Tech in Ruston, Grambling University in Grambling, and Northwestern State University in Natchitoches. Of course, for those willing to travel to South Louisiana, there's nothing like LSU and Tiger Stadium on a Saturday night. Known throughout college football as "Death Valley," it is rumored that thunderous fans once caused an earth tremor that registered on a seismograph across campus in the Department of Geology.

Finally, you can head to Harrah's Louisiana Downs in Bossier City for the SUPER DERBY FESTIVAL OF RACING. This is a month-long extravaganza that has more than twenty fun-filled events, the proceeds from which go to benefit nonprofit organizations. The festival culminates with the running of the Super Derby, a race that attracts some of the best three-year-old thoroughbreds in the country.

However you choose to celebrate in the month of September, you'll always win in Northwest Louisiana.

BRANDY SMASHERS

Serves 20

ingredients

2 cups sugar
2 cups water
1 (12-ounce) can frozen orange
   juice concentrate
1 (12-ounce) can frozen
   lemonade concentrate
1 pint brandy

method

Combine the sugar and water in a saucepan and mix well. Bring to a boil and boil until the sugar dissolves, stirring occasionally. Remove from the heat and stir in the orange juice concentrate, lemonade concentrate and brandy. Pour the brandy mixture into a large freezer container and freeze until slushy. Spoon into glasses.

BROWN SUGAR BRIE

Serves 8

ingredients

1 (8-ounce) round Brie cheese
1½ cups packed brown sugar
½ cup (1 stick) butter
Chopped pecans

method

Remove the rind from the top of the Brie, leaving a 1-inch border. Arrange the round on a baking sheet. Combine the brown sugar and butter in a saucepan and cook until blended, stirring frequently. Stir in the pecans.

Spread the brown sugar mixture over the top of the round and bake at 325 degrees for 10 minutes or until heated through and bubbly. Serve with assorted party crackers and/or sliced apples.

CROSTINI WITH GOAT CHEESE AND MUSHROOMS

Makes 2 dozen

ingredients

CROSTINI
1 baguette French bread, cut
    diagonally into 1/4-inch slices
Extra-virgin olive oil

MUSHROOM TOPPING
  AND ASSEMBLY
1 tablespoon extra-virgin olive oil
2 cups coarsely chopped
    mushrooms (shiitake, cremini
    and/or button)
2 garlic cloves, minced
1/2 teaspoon kosher salt
Freshly ground pepper to taste
8 ounces herb-seasoned
    goat cheese
Sprigs of thyme

method

CROSTINI
Lightly brush both sides of the baguette slices with olive oil or spray with olive oil nonstick cooking spray. Arrange the slices in a single layer on a baking sheet and bake at 375 degrees for 8 to 10 minutes or until crisp. Remove to a wire rack to cool.

TOPPING
Heat the olive oil in a skillet over medium-low heat and add the mushrooms, garlic, salt and pepper. Sauté for 5 to 10 minutes or until the mushrooms have released their juices and are tender. Remove from the heat.

ASSEMBLY
Spread each crostini with goat cheese and top evenly with the sautéed mushroom mixture. Arrange on a serving platter and garnish with sprigs of thyme.

*B*eer will stay colder longer in a bottle than in a can. Aluminum cans are very thin, so when you hold the can it is easy for the heat from your hands to transfer to the can and lower the temperature of the beer. A glass bottle, however, is much thicker. Thus, the heat from your hands cannot penetrate as well, and the beer will stay colder much longer.

SUPERIOR GRILL'S CHILI CON QUESO*

Makes about 8 cups

ingredients

¼ cup (½ stick) butter
2 tablespoons chopped onion
2 tablespoons all-purpose flour
1 (8-ounce) can peeled tomatoes,
   drained
1 jalapeño chile, or to taste, chopped
2 (12-ounce) cans evaporated milk
6 to 8 cups (24 to 32 ounces)
   shredded Monterey Jack cheese

*Photograph for this recipe on page 141.

method

Cook the butter and onion in a large saucepan until the butter melts, stirring constantly. Add the flour and mix until combined. Stir in the tomatoes, jalapeño chile and evaporated milk and cook until heated through, stirring frequently; do not boil. Remove from the heat and add the cheese, stirring until melted.

APPLE DIP

Serves 16

ingredients

16 ounces cream cheese, softened
1 cup packed brown sugar
¾ cup granulated sugar
1½ teaspoons vanilla extract
1 package toffee bits
Apple wedges

method

Beat the cream cheese, brown sugar, granulated sugar and vanilla in a mixing bowl until creamy, scraping the bowl occasionally. Chill, covered, for 8 to 10 hours. Stir in the toffee bits and serve with apple wedges and/or fresh fruit of choice.

HARVEST MUFFINS*

Feel free to cut this recipe in half. You can also bake these muffins in miniature muffin cups.

Makes 3 dozen

ingredients

4 cups all-purpose flour
2 1/2 cups sugar
4 teaspoons baking soda
4 teaspoons ground cinnamon
1 teaspoon salt
6 eggs
2 cups canola oil
4 teaspoons vanilla extract
4 cups grated carrots
1 cup raisins
1 cup flaked coconut
2 apples, peeled and grated

*Photograph for this recipe on page 141.

method

Sift the flour, sugar, baking soda, cinnamon and salt into a bowl and mix well. Beat the eggs in a mixing bowl until blended. Add the canola oil and vanilla and beat until combined. Add the flour mixture and mix just until moistened. Fold in the carrots, raisins, coconut and apples and spoon the batter evenly into muffin cups sprayed with nonstick cooking spray.

Bake at 350 degrees for 20 minutes or until the tops of the muffins spring back when lightly touched. Cool in the pans for 5 minutes and remove to a wire rack to cool completely.

To ensure that your breads, cakes, or muffins do not turn out flat, check the potency of your baking powder before you bake. Mix one teaspoon of baking powder with one-third cup of hot water. If the mixture bubbles vigorously, it is fine. If not, purchase new baking powder for your recipe.

CHOCOLATE ZUCCHINI BREAD

Makes 1 loaf

ingredients

2 cups all-purpose flour

2 tablespoons baking cocoa

1¼ teaspoons baking soda

1 teaspoon ground cinnamon

¼ teaspoon salt

¾ cup sugar

3 tablespoons canola oil

2 eggs

1 cup applesauce

1½ cups finely shredded zucchini

½ cup (3 ounces) semisweet
   chocolate chips

method

Mix the flour, baking cocoa, baking soda, cinnamon and salt in a bowl. Combine the sugar, canola oil and eggs in a mixing bowl and beat at low speed until blended. Stir in the applesauce. Add the flour mixture and beat just until moistened. Fold in the zucchini and chocolate chips.

Spoon the batter into a 5×9-inch loaf pan coated with nonstick cooking spray. Bake at 350 degrees for 1 hour or until a wooden pick inserted in the center comes out almost clean. Cool in the pan on a wire rack for 10 minutes. Remove to the wire rack to cool completely.

*M*any celebrated sports figures have called Shreveport home at one time or another, including Terry Bradshaw, Karl Malone, David Toms, and Hal Sutton.

PEAR AND BLUE CHEESE SALAD

Serves 6 to 8

ingredients

RASPBERRY VINAIGRETTE
1/4 cup raspberry vinegar
1 tablespoon Dijon mustard
1 teaspoon sugar
1/2 cup extra-virgin olive oil
Salt and pepper to taste

SALAD
1 package spring mix salad greens
1 cup chopped Bosc pear
4 ounces blue cheese, crumbled
1/4 cup chopped walnuts

method

VINAIGRETTE

Whisk the vinegar, Dijon mustard and sugar in a bowl until blended. Add the olive oil gradually, whisking constantly until the oil is incorporated. Season with salt and pepper.

SALAD

Toss the salad greens, pear and cheese in a salad bowl. Add the vinaigrette and mix gently until coated. Sprinkle with the walnuts.

*M*aytag blue cheese is one of the finest blue cheeses in the world. Produced from the freshest unpasteurized milk obtainable from only two herds of Holstein cows located near Newton, Iowa, its moisture content is higher than that of most other blue cheeses, making it very creamy and spreadable.

APPLE SLAW*

Serves 8

ingredients

SWEET SLAW VINAIGRETTE
1/3 cup packed brown sugar
1/3 cup cider vinegar
1 1/2 tablespoons canola oil
1/4 teaspoon salt
1/4 teaspoon freshly ground pepper

SLAW
1 (12-ounce) package broccoli slaw
2 1/2 cups chopped sweet apples
1 (3-ounce) package dried tart
   cherries or craisins
2 tablespoons sunflower seeds

*Photograph for this recipe on page 141.

method

VINAIGRETTE
Whisk the brown sugar, vinegar, canola oil, salt and pepper in a bowl until combined

SLAW
Toss the broccoli slaw, apples and cherries in a salad bowl. Add the vinaigrette and mix until coated. Sprinkle with the sunflower seeds. Chill, covered, for up to 3 hours.

FALL BEAN SALAD*

Green beans and wax beans are crisp and snappy. To retain their bright color, cook them until they are al dente and dress them just before serving.

Serves 8

ingredients

1 1/2 pounds tender green
   beans, trimmed
1 1/2 pounds tender wax
   beans, trimmed
Salt to taste
1/4 cup extra-virgin olive oil
2 tablespoons minced shallots
Freshly ground pepper to taste
Splash of fresh lemon juice or red
   wine vinegar
1/2 cup torn fresh basil leaves
4 ounces blue cheese,
   crumbled (optional)

*Photograph for this recipe on page 141.

method

Cook the green beans and wax beans in boiling salted water in a saucepan for 4 to 5 minutes or until tender-crisp. Drain and immediately rinse with cold water to stop the cooking process. Drain again and pat dry with paper towels.

Toss the beans, olive oil and shallots in a large bowl. Season with salt and pepper. Just before serving, toss with the lemon juice and basil and sprinkle with the cheese. Serve immediately. If wax beans are not available, just use additional green beans.

ROASTED ROSEMARY POTATO SALAD*

Serves 6

ingredients

2¹/2 pounds small red new potatoes

1 red onion, cut into wedges

2 tablespoons olive oil

2 tablespoons chopped
   fresh rosemary

2 garlic cloves, minced

¹/2 teaspoon salt

¹/2 teaspoon freshly ground pepper

2 tablespoons balsamic vinegar

2 tablespoons olive oil

1 red bell pepper, cut into
   small chunks

3 tablespoons pine nuts, toasted

*Photograph for this recipe on page 141.

method

Toss the potatoes, onion, 2 tablespoons olive oil, the rosemary, garlic, salt and pepper in a shallow baking pan until coated and spread in a single layer. Roast at 450 degrees for 25 to 30 minutes or until light brown, stirring occasionally. Spoon the potato mixture into a bowl.

Whisk the vinegar and 2 tablespoons olive oil in a small bowl until blended and pour over the potato mixture. Add the bell pepper and toss to coat. Sprinkle with the pine nuts and serve warm or at room temperature.

When tailgating, discard perishable foods that have sat out in temperatures over ninety degrees for more than an hour, or for more than two hours in moderate weather. To be safe, follow the rule, "When in doubt, throw it out."

ROASTED RED PEPPER BISQUE

. . . .

A mixture of puréed onion, garlic and roasted red peppers makes a
great spread with goat cheese and crackers.

Serves 4

ingredients

ROASTED BELL PEPPERS
5 large red bell peppers
3 tablespoons olive oil

SOUP
2 tablespoons olive oil
1 large onion, chopped
2 garlic cloves, crushed
3/4 teaspoon ground cumin
2 (14-ounce) cans chicken broth
1 to 2 tablespoons fresh lime juice
Salt and freshly ground pepper
　to taste
1/4 cup sour cream
Chopped fresh cilantro

method

PEPPERS
Brush the bell peppers with the olive oil and arrange in a single layer on a baking sheet. Roast at 500 degrees for 20 minutes or until the skin is blistered and charred, turning several times. Immediately place the bell peppers in a sealable plastic bag and seal tightly. Let steam for 30 minutes. Peel, seed and coarsely chop the roasted peppers; rinse the peppers at this point, if desired. You may freeze for future use.

SOUP
Heat the olive oil in a large saucepan and add the onion and garlic. Sauté until the onion is tender and stir in the cumin. Cook for 1 to 2 minutes or until the onion is coated and the mixture is fragrant. Stir in the roasted bell peppers and broth.

Simmer, uncovered, for 10 minutes, stirring occasionally. Process the soup in batches in a food processor until smooth and stir in the lime juice. Season with salt and pepper and stir in the sour cream. Serve hot or chilled in soup bowls. Garnish each serving with cilantro.

Nutritionally speaking, red bell peppers are superior by quite a bit. They are eleven times higher in beta carotene and have one and one-half times more vitamin C than green bell peppers. Although hot red chiles contain fourteen times more beta carotene than hot green chiles, their vitamin C content is the same.

ALL-TIME FAVORITE BROCCOLI CASSEROLE

Serves 4

ingredients

1 (16-ounce) package frozen
  broccoli florets
8 ounces Cheddar cheese,
  shredded
1/2 (10-ounce) can cream of
  mushroom soup
1/2 cup mayonnaise
1 egg, beaten
1/2 (16-ounce) package herb-
  seasoned stuffing mix
1/2 cup (1 stick) butter, melted

method

Cook the broccoli using the package directions for 5 minutes and drain. Combine one-half of the cheese, the soup, mayonnaise and egg in a bowl and mix well. Fold in the broccoli and spoon into a baking dish sprayed with nonstick cooking spray. Sprinkle with the remaining cheese and the stuffing mix. Drizzle with the butter and bake at 350 degrees for 20 minutes.

LONDON GRILL*

This fantastic, easy recipe is a favorite with family and guests. Serve hot or chilled. Leftovers make a terrific po-boy with thinly sliced beef, garlic mayonnaise, herbed tomatoes, and lettuce.

Serves 6

ingredients

1 tablespoon olive oil
2 teaspoons chopped fresh parsley
1 garlic clove, crushed
1 teaspoon salt
1 teaspoon lemon juice
1/8 teaspoon pepper
11/2 to 2 pounds flank steak

*Photograph for this recipe on page 141.

method

Whisk the olive oil, parsley, garlic, salt, lemon juice and pepper in a bowl. Brush both sides of the steak with the olive oil mixture and place in a shallow dish.

Marinate, covered, in the refrigerator for 30 minutes to several hours. Grill over hot coals for 7 minutes per side. Cut across the grain into thin slices.

BEEF LOMBARDI

Serves 6

ingredients

1 pound lean ground beef
1 (14-ounce) can chopped tomatoes
1 (10-ounce) can tomatoes with
    green chiles
2 teaspoons sugar
2 teaspoons salt
1/4 teaspoon pepper
1 (6-ounce) can tomato paste
1 bay leaf
6 ounces medium egg noodles
6 green onions, chopped
    (about 1/2 cup)
1 cup sour cream
1 cup (4 ounces) shredded sharp
    Cheddar cheese
1 cup (4 ounces) shredded
    Parmesan cheese
1 cup (4 ounces) shredded
    mozzarella cheese

method

Cook the ground beef in a skillet over medium heat for 5 to 6 minutes or until brown and crumbly; drain. Stir in the undrained tomatoes, undrained tomatoes with green chiles, sugar, salt and pepper. Cook for 5 minutes and stir in the tomato paste and bay leaf.

Simmer for 30 minutes, stirring occasionally. Cook the pasta using the package directions and drain. Mix the pasta, green onions and sour cream in a bowl and spread over the bottom of a lightly greased 9×13-inch baking dish. Top with the ground beef mixture and sprinkle with the Cheddar cheese, Parmesan cheese and mozzarella cheese.

Bake, covered with foil, at 350 degrees for 35 minutes. Remove the foil and bake for 5 minutes longer. You may freeze the unbaked dish for up to one month. Thaw in the refrigerator and bake as directed above.

The best way to fast-chill beer is to plunge it into a cooler chest filled with water and ice. The beer will be ice cold in about twenty minutes. The ice water absorbs the warmth from the bottle faster and more efficiently than the cold air of your refrigerator can.

NATCHITOCHES MEAT PIES*

Makes 32 meat pies

ingredients

MEAT FILLING

2 1/2 pounds ground beef

1 1/2 pounds bulk pork sausage

2 large onions, chopped

1 bell pepper, chopped

2 bunches green onions, trimmed
    and chopped

2 ribs celery, chopped

3 tablespoons chopped fresh parsley

1 tablespoon salt

2 teaspoons black pepper

2 teaspoons red pepper flakes

2 garlic cloves, minced

3 tablespoons all-purpose flour

PASTRY

5 cups all-purpose flour

2 1/2 teaspoons salt

2 1/2 teaspoons baking powder

3/4 cup shortening

3/4 cup milk

2 eggs

Vegetable oil for frying

*Photograph for this recipe on page 141.

FILLING

Brown the ground beef and sausage in a large skillet, stirring until crumbly; drain. Stir in the onions, bell pepper, green onions, celery, parsley, salt, black pepper, red pepper flakes and garlic. Cook for 40 to 45 minutes or until the ground beef and sausage are cooked through but not dry, stirring frequently. Remove from the heat and stir in the flour. Let stand until cool.

PASTRY

Sift the flour, salt and baking powder into a large bowl and mix well. Cut in the shortening until crumbly. Whisk the milk and eggs in a bowl until blended. Add the milk mixture to the flour mixture gradually and stir until a stiff dough forms.

Roll the dough thin on a lightly floured surface and cut into 5-inch rounds. Spoon some of the ground beef mixture on one-half of each round. Dampen the edges of the rounds with water and fold over to cover the filling, sealing the edges with a fork dipped in additional flour. You may chill or freeze the pies at this point. Just before serving, fry the pies in oil in a deep skillet for several minutes or until golden brown on both sides and drain. Serve immediately.

BARBECUED CHICKEN POTPIE

Serves 8

ingredients

1 tablespoon butter

2 cups chopped onions

1/2 cup chopped bell pepper

1/3 cup chopped seeded poblano
   chile, or 1 can chopped
   green chiles

1 garlic clove, minced

1 1/2 teaspoons cumin seeds

1 teaspoon coriander

1/4 cup cider vinegar

4 cups shredded cooked chicken

1 (14-ounce) can chicken broth

1 (12-ounce) bottle chili sauce

3 tablespoons brown sugar

1 ounce chocolate, grated

1 can refrigerator corn bread twists

method

Melt the butter in a large skillet and add the onions, bell pepper, poblano chile and garlic. Sauté for 5 minutes and stir in the cumin seeds and coriander. Cook for 2 minutes and stir in the vinegar, scraping the bottom of the skillet to dislodge any browned bits. Add the chicken, broth, chili sauce, brown sugar and chocolate and mix well.

Cook for 15 minutes or until thickened, stirring occasionally. Spoon the chicken mixture into a 9×13-inch baking dish sprayed with nonstick cooking spray. Separate the corn bread twists and arrange lattice-fashion over the top of the prepared layer. Bake at 375 degrees for 25 minutes. Let stand for 15 minutes before serving.

FRESH APPLE CAKE*

- -

Serves 16

ingredients

2 cups chopped peeled apples
   or pears
1/2 cup granulated sugar
1/2 cup packed brown sugar
1 cup all-purpose flour
1/2 cup self-rising flour
2 teaspoons ground cinnamon
1 teaspoon baking soda
1/2 teaspoon salt
3/4 cup vegetable oil
2 eggs, beaten
1 teaspoon vanilla extract
3/4 cup chopped pecans
3/4 cup raisins

*Photograph for this recipe on page 141.

method

Toss the apples, granulated sugar and brown sugar in a bowl. Let stand at room temperature for 1 hour. Mix the all-purpose flour, self-rising flour, cinnamon, baking soda and salt in a bowl. Stir the oil, eggs and vanilla into the apple mixture. Add the flour mixture and mix well. Stir in the pecans and raisins.

Spoon the batter into a greased and floured bundt pan and bake at 325 degrees for 1 hour. Cool in the pan for 10 minutes. Remove to a wire rack to cool completely. You may bake in muffin cups, if desired.

In 1974, the Junior League provided funds to start the Rutherford House, a residential treatment center for eight to ten girls between the ages of twelve and seventeen, who had come to the attention of the juvenile courts in the Shreveport area for indulging in behavior detrimental to their well-being and mental growth. Over the next two years, the house expanded to include the Olive House Branch for ten boys and Rutherford House II for twelve more girls. The children were kept for four months, with follow-up help provided indefinitely.

HONEY BUN CAKE

This delicious cake is great for the men in your life to take to the hunting camp. They will love it.

Serves 15

CAKE

1 (2-layer) yellow cake mix
1 cup sour cream
2/3 cup vegetable oil
4 eggs
1 cup packed brown sugar
1 tablespoon ground cinnamon

CONFECTIONERS' SUGAR ICING

3 cups confectioners' sugar
1/2 cup milk
1 teaspoon vanilla extract

CAKE

Combine the cake mix, sour cream, oil and eggs in a mixing bowl and beat until blended. Spread one-half of the batter in a 9×13-inch cake pan. Sprinkle with a mixture of the brown sugar and cinnamon and spread with the remaining batter. Swirl with a knife and bake at 325 degrees for 40 minutes. Cool in the pan on a wire rack.

ICING

Mix the confectioners' sugar, milk and vanilla in a bowl until of the desired consistency. Spread the icing over the top of the cake. Let stand until set.

"EVERYTHING BUT THE KITCHEN SINK" BAR COOKIES*

Makes 3 dozen bars

1 (18-ounce) roll refrigerator
    chocolate chip cookie dough
1 (7-ounce) jar marshmallow creme
1/2 cup creamy peanut butter
1 1/2 cups corn Chex
1/2 cup "M & M's" Chocolate Candies

*Photograph for this recipe on page 141.

Pat the cookie dough over the bottom of a greased 9×13-inch baking pan. Bake at 350 degrees for 13 minutes. Drop teaspoonfuls of the marshmallow creme and peanut butter over the top of the baked layer and bake for 1 minute.

Carefully spread the melted marshmallow creme and peanut butter over the top. Sprinkle with the cereal and chocolate candies and bake for 7 minutes longer. Cool in the pan on a wire rack and cut into 2-inch bars.

OCTOBER

The shorter days and cool, crisp nights of October

tell us that autumn has arrived. For area

red river revel arts festival

residents, this time of year also marks the arrival

state fair of louisiana

of the Red River Revel, the Louisiana State Fair,

pumpkin shine on line

and, of course, Halloween.

monterey days heritage festival

*S*horter days and cooler nights have definitely arrived with October, and in Northwest Louisiana, the month is filled with time-honored celebrations that hold special significance to area residents.

Shreveport boasts THE RED RIVER REVEL ARTS FESTIVAL, an eight-day event that includes hundreds of the country's top artists, craftsmen, entertainers, and culinary masters. The festival is the largest arts festival in the south and was proudly given to the city as a bicentennial gift from the Junior League of Shreveport-Bossier in 1976. It is undeniably one of the most cherished and most successful festivals in the state, and it has also garnered considerable national recognition, having been featured on ABC's *Good Morning America!*, named as one of the "Top 100 Fine-Arts Festivals" in *Sunshine Artists Magazine*, and named as one of the Top 20 events by the Southeastern Tourism Society. You'll also find a remarkable variety of delicious food, hands-on activities for children, and big-name live entertainment.

In October people from all over the state and beyond travel to Shreveport to attend the STATE FAIR OF LOUISIANA. It serves as the official State Fair for Louisiana, though it has no formal ties to either the city or state. It was founded by a group of Shreveport's leading citizens in 1906 and is now run by a private, not-for-profit organization representing a broad cross section of Louisiana. The Fair has always paid tribute to Louisiana's farming and livestock traditions, and these traditions are still honored today. Prejudged competitive exhibits feature prize-winning canned goods, arts and crafts, photography, and much more. Of course, the two-week-long celebration also has plenty of food and the ever-popular carnival rides.

In addition to these two big-name events, October also claims several smaller festivals in the region. At the ROBELINE HERITAGE FESTIVAL you can discover how this community became known as "Robbers Lane" and celebrate the history and heritage of the nearby Los Adaes State Commemorative area, once the capital of Spanish Texas Territory for more than 50 years. Mooringsport has its two-day FALL FESTIVAL to celebrate the season, while Vivian has its MONTEREY DAYS HERITAGE FESTIVAL to celebrate the local folklore. Shreveport hosts PIONEER HERITAGE DAYS on the campus of LSUS, an event where the history of some of the area's earliest settlers comes to life with demonstrations of blacksmithing, quilting, arrowhead making, and more.

The Red River Revel Arts Festival

Finally, like people all over America, Northwest Louisiana also celebrates the traditions of HALLOWEEN. One favorite local event in Shreveport is the PUMPKIN SHINE ON LINE, where you can see pumpkin after creative pumpkin decorated by individuals, families, and local school classes as you wind along the trails of Betty Virginia Park.

As the month of October comes to an end, the stage is set for the two remaining months of the year, when our hearts and minds are filled with holiday spirit.

AUTUMN HOT CRANBERRY CITRUS PUNCH

Serves 12 to 15

ingredients

1 (32-ounce) bottle cranberry juice
2 cups orange juice
1/2 cup lemon juice
1/2 cup honey
1/4 cup lime juice
3 whole cloves
2 cinnamon sticks
1 (32-ounce) bottle ginger ale
Cinnamon sticks (optional)

method

Combine the cranberry juice, orange juice, lemon juice, honey, lime juice, cloves and 2 cinnamon sticks in a stockpot. Simmer over medium heat for about 15 minutes, stirring occasionally. Discard the cloves and cinnamon sticks. Just before serving, mix in the ginger ale and simmer until warm. Serve hot in heated mugs. Garnish each serving with a cinnamon stick, if desired.

WITCHES' BREW

Add dry ice to the punch for a creepy Halloween effect.
Makes about 13 cups

ingredients

1/3 cup water
1/3 cup sugar
2 cinnamon sticks
5 whole cloves
3 tablespoons finely chopped
  fresh ginger
1 (25-ounce) bottle sparkling
  cider, chilled
1 (1-quart) bottle cranberry juice
  cocktail, chilled
1 (1-liter) bottle club soda or seltzer
  water, chilled
1 cup dark rum (optional)
Ice blocks in any shape

method

Combine the water, sugar, cinnamon sticks, cloves and ginger in a saucepan and mix well. Bring to a boil and boil until the sugar dissolves, stirring frequently. Reduce the heat to low and simmer, covered, for 5 minutes. Remove from the heat and let stand until cool. You may store the syrup, covered, in the refrigerator for up to 1 week.

Mix the sparkling cider, cranberry juice cocktail, club soda and rum in a punch bowl. Strain the cooled syrup into the punch mixture and mix well, discarding the solids. Add the ice blocks. Ladle into punch cups.

MONSTER EYEBALLS

Makes 100

1 pound hot bulk pork sausage

10 ounces extra-sharp Cheddar
    cheese, shredded

3 cups baking mix

100 pimento-stuffed green olives

Mix the sausage and cheese in a large mixing bowl until combined. Add the baking mix gradually, mixing well after each addition. Shape the sausage mixture into small balls. Stuff 1 olive into each ball and reshape the sausage mixture to enclose the olive, leaving the pimento end exposed. Cover the olive completely if you do not want the "eyeball" effect.

Arrange the sausage balls on a lightly greased baking sheet. Bake at 350 degrees for 15 minutes or until light brown. You may freeze the unbaked sausage balls for future use. Freeze on a baking sheet and transfer to a sealable freezer bag. Thaw in the refrigerator and bake as directed above.

ROASTED BUTTERNUT SQUASH DIP

Makes 4 cups

1 (2-pound) butternut squash

1 small sweet onion, quartered

4 unpeeled garlic cloves

$1\frac{1}{2}$ teaspoons olive oil

2 tablespoons sour cream

$3/4$ teaspoon salt

$1/8$ teaspoon ground red pepper

$1/8$ teaspoon freshly ground
    black pepper

Cut the squash lengthwise into halves and discard the seeds and membranes. Brush the cut sides of the squash halves, cut sides of the onion quarters and the garlic cloves with the olive oil.

Arrange the squash cut side down, the onion quarters and garlic on a baking sheet and roast at 350 degrees for 45 minutes or until tender. Cool slightly and peel the squash. Squeeze the garlic cloves to extract the pulp. Combine the squash, onion and garlic pulp in a food processor and process until smooth. Add the sour cream, salt, red pepper and black pepper and process until combined. Serve warm with chips.

PUMPKIN DIP

Serves 12

ingredients

6 ounces cream cheese, softened
1/2 cup packed brown sugar
1/2 cup canned pumpkin
2 teaspoons maple syrup
1/2 teaspoon ground cinnamon
Apple slices

method

Combine the cream cheese, brown sugar and pumpkin in a mixing bowl and beat at medium speed until blended. Add the syrup and cinnamon and beat until smooth. Chill, covered, for 30 minutes. Serve with apple slices or soft gingersnap cookies.

GOOD MORNING PUMPKIN PANCAKES

Makes 16 pancakes

ingredients

2 cups baking mix
1 (12-ounce) can evaporated milk
1/2 cup pumpkin
2 eggs, lightly beaten
2 tablespoons light brown sugar
2 tablespoons vegetable oil
2 teaspoons ground cinnamon
1 teaspoon ground allspice
1 teaspoon vanilla extract

method

Combine the baking mix, evaporated milk, pumpkin, eggs, brown sugar, oil, cinnamon, allspice and vanilla in a medium bowl and mix until smooth; do not overmix. Pour 1/4 cup of the batter per pancake onto a hot lightly greased griddle and cook until the edges are dry. Turn and cook until golden brown.

You may prepare the pancakes in advance and freeze them for future use. Cook the pancakes as directed above and let stand until cool. Arrange the pancakes in a single layer on a baking sheet and freeze until firm. Store the frozen pancakes in a sealable freezer bag in the freezer until ready to use. Microwave just before serving.

BUTTERNUT SQUASH BISQUE

Serves 8

ingredients

1 (3-pound) butternut squash
2¹/2 tablespoons butter
1 large onion, chopped
3¹/2 cups chicken broth
2 large tart apples, peeled
    and chopped
1 large Bartlett pear, peeled
    and chopped
2 tablespoons chopped fresh thyme,
    or 2 teaspoons dried thyme
1 tablespoon chopped fresh sage,
    or 1 teaspoon dried sage
1 bay leaf
¹/2 teaspoon salt
¹/2 teaspoon pepper
¹/2 to 1 cup half-and-half

method

Cut the squash lengthwise into halves and discard the seeds. Peel with a vegetable peeler and cut into 1¹/2-inch chunks. Melt the butter in a 4-quart saucepan over medium-high heat and add the onion. Sauté for 4 minutes or until tender. Stir in the squash, broth, apples and pear. Add the thyme, sage, bay leaf, salt and pepper and mix well.

Bring the squash mixture to a boil over medium-high heat and reduce the heat to low. Simmer for 20 minutes or until the squash is tender, stirring occasionally. Cool to room temperature and discard the bay leaf.

Process the squash mixture in batches in a food processor until puréed. Pour the purée into a clean saucepan and stir in the half-and-half. Simmer just until heated through; do not boil. Ladle into soup bowls.

For a festive serving container, hollow out a large pumpkin for the soup tureen. Serve in smaller ornamental pumpkins by slicing off the tops and hollowing out the pulp. Rub the inside with oil, salt and pepper and ladle the hot bisque into the pumpkin shells. Top with the pumpkin lids and arrange on serving plates.

BLUE CHEESE TWICE-BAKED POTATOES

Serves 4

ingredients

4 baking potatoes
Vegetable oil
1/2 cup sour cream
2 to 3 ounces blue cheese, crumbled
1/4 cup milk
1/4 cup (1/2 stick) butter, softened
3/4 teaspoon salt
1/8 teaspoon pepper
Crumbled crisp-cooked bacon

method

Coat the potatoes with oil and arrange on a baking sheet. Bake at 400 degrees for 1 1/2 hours or until tender. Maintain the oven temperature. Cool the potatoes slightly and cut a thin lengthwise slice from the top of each potato. Remove the pulp, leaving a shell. Mash the potato pulp in a mixing bowl. Add the sour cream, cheese, milk, butter, salt and pepper to the potato pulp and beat until fluffy. Spoon the potato mixture into the potato shells and arrange the potatoes on a baking sheet. Bake for 15 minutes or until heated through. Sprinkle with bacon and serve immediately.

SAUSAGE-STUFFED ACORN SQUASH

Serves 6

ingredients

3 acorn squash
1 pound hot bulk pork sausage
1 small onion, chopped
2 garlic cloves, minced
2 cups (8 ounces) shredded
    mozzarella cheese, divided
1 cup cottage cheese
1/2 cup fresh bread crumbs
1/4 cup chopped fresh parsley
1 1/4 teaspoons oregano
1/2 teaspoon salt
1/2 teaspoon red pepper
1/4 cup chopped fresh parsley

method

Cut the squash crosswise into halves and remove the seeds. Arrange the squash cut sides down in a baking dish. Add just enough hot water to cover the bottom of the dish. Bake, covered with foil, at 350 degrees for 30 minutes or until tender. Remove the squash to a platter to cool. Brown the sausage with the onion and garlic in a skillet over medium heat, stirring until the sausage is crumbly; drain. Combine the sausage mixture, 1 cup mozzarella cheese, the cottage cheese, bread crumbs, 1/4 cup parsley, the oregano, salt and red pepper in a bowl and mix well. Spoon the sausage mixture into the squash halves and arrange in a baking dish. Mix the remaining 1 cup mozzarella cheese and 1/4 cup parsley in a bowl and sprinkle over the top. Bake at 375 degrees for 5 minutes.

SQUASH POTATO CASSEROLE

Serves 6 to 8

ingredients

6 yellow squash, sliced
4 large potatoes, sliced
1/2 onion, sliced
8 ounces Cheddar cheese, shredded
1/2 cup (1 stick) butter, softened
3 eggs, lightly beaten
1 sleeve saltine crackers, crushed
Salt and pepper to taste

method

Combine the squash, potatoes and onion with enough water to cover in a saucepan. Bring to a boil and boil until the vegetables are tender; drain. Combine the squash mixture, one-half of the cheese, the butter, eggs, crackers, salt and pepper in a bowl and mix well.

Spoon the squash mixture into a 9×13-inch baking dish sprayed with nonstick cooking spray. Sprinkle with the remaining cheese and bake at 375 degrees for 30 minutes.

JACK-O'-LANTERN CHEESEBURGER PIE

Serves 6 to 8

ingredients

1 pound ground beef
1 onion, chopped
2 garlic cloves, crushed
3/4 teaspoon salt
1/2 teaspoon pepper
3 cups (12 ounces) shredded
   Monterey Jack cheese, divided
1/4 cup ketchup
1 teaspoon Worcestershire sauce
2 refrigerator pie crusts
1 tablespoon prepared mustard
2 tablespoons water
1 drop of red food coloring
1 drop of yellow food coloring
1 egg, beaten

method

Brown the ground beef with the onion, garlic, salt and pepper in a skillet, stirring until crumbly; drain. Stir in 2 cups cheese, the ketchup and Worcestershire sauce. Place one of the pie crusts on a lightly greased baking sheet and spread with the prepared mustard. Spread the ground beef mixture over the mustard, leaving a 2-inch border.

Place the remaining pie crust on a hard surface and cut out a jack-o'-lantern face. Place the pie crust over the ground beef mixture. Crimp the edge of the pie crust and fold under. Whisk the water and food coloring in a bowl and brush over the pie crust.

Bake at 425 degrees for 20 minutes. Remove from the oven and brush with the egg. Fill the eyes, nose and mouth with the remaining 1 cup cheese and bake for 5 to 10 minutes longer or until golden brown.

HONEY GARLIC PORK TENDERLOIN

Serves 6

ingredients

MARINADE AND PORK
1/2 cup Creole mustard
1/2 cup honey
2 tablespoons lemon juice
8 garlic cloves, minced
2 teaspoons salt
2 teaspoons pepper
2 pounds pork tenderloin

HONEY-CREOLE SAUCE
1/2 cup Creole mustard
1/3 cup mayonnaise
1/4 cup honey
1 tablespoon lemon juice
1/2 teaspoon pepper

method

MARINADE AND PORK

Mix the Creole mustard, honey, lemon juice, garlic, salt and pepper in a large shallow dish or sealable heavy-duty plastic bag. Add the pork and turn to coat. Cover or seal tightly and marinate in the refrigerator for 3 to 10 hours, turning occasionally; drain.

Place the pork on a lightly greased rack in a foil-lined roasting pan. Broil 6 inches from the heat source for 5 minutes. Roast at 425 degrees for 15 minutes or until a meat thermometer inserted in the thickest portion registers 160 degrees. Let stand for several minutes before slicing.

SAUCE

Mix the Creole mustard, mayonnaise, honey, lemon juice and pepper in a bowl until of a sauce consistency. Serve the sauce with the pork.

The Professional Women's Group is a job retention component of the Dress for Success program. This group is designed for the women suited by Dress for Success who have entered or reentered the work force. Educational topics such as workplace etiquette, computer skills, child care options, and managing finances are provided, as well as other relevant topics. Networking opportunities are another benefit to the women learning to live independently through this project. The League began facilitating this program in 2003.

CREAMY CHICKEN LASAGNA

Serves 8 to 10

ingredients

4 boneless skinless chicken breasts,
  boiled or poached
9 lasagna noodles
1 tablespoon butter or margarine
8 ounces fresh mushrooms, sliced
1/3 cup butter
1/3 cup all-purpose flour
3 cups milk
1 1/2 cups (6 ounces) freshly grated
  Parmesan cheese
1/2 cup heavy cream
3/4 teaspoon basil
1/2 teaspoon salt
1/4 teaspoon freshly ground pepper
Chopped fresh parsley
Paprika to taste

method

Chop the chicken into bite-size pieces and place in a large bowl. Cook the pasta using the package directions and drain. Arrange the pasta in a single layer on a sheet of waxed paper.

Melt 1 tablespoon butter in a large skillet over medium-high heat and add the mushrooms. Cook until tender, stirring constantly. Drain and add to the bowl containing the chicken. Melt 1/3 cup butter in a skillet and mix in the flour. Cook for 1 minute, stirring constantly. Add the milk gradually, stirring constantly. Cook for 3 minutes or until bubbly. Stir in the cheese, heavy cream, basil, salt and pepper. Cook until the cheese melts and the mixture thickens, stirring frequently. Stir the chicken mixture into the cheese mixture.

Layer the chicken mixture and noodles one-third at a time in a 9×13-inch baking dish sprayed with nonstick cooking spray. Bake, covered, at 350 degrees for 30 minutes. Let stand for 10 minutes and sprinkle with parsley and paprika.

BUTTERMILK BAKED CHICKEN

Delicious home cooking. Serve any extra sauce over mashed potatoes.

Serves 4

ingredients

1/4 cup (1/2 stick) butter
4 boneless skinless chicken breasts
1/2 teaspoon salt
1/2 teaspoon pepper
1/2 cup buttermilk
3/4 cup all-purpose flour
1 (10-ounce) can cream of
  mushroom soup
1 cup buttermilk

method

Melt the butter in a lightly greased 9×13-inch baking dish in a 425-degree oven. Maintain the oven temperature. Sprinkle the chicken with the salt and pepper and dip in 1/2 cup buttermilk. Coat with the flour and arrange the chicken in a single layer in the prepared baking dish. Bake for 15 minutes and turn. Bake for 10 minutes. Mix the soup and 1 cup buttermilk in a bowl and pour over the chicken. Bake, covered with foil, for 10 minutes longer.

PUMPKIN PIE CAKE

Serves 15

ingredients

4 eggs
1 1/2 cups sugar
1 teaspoon ground cinnamon
1/4 teaspoon ground nutmeg
1/4 teaspoon pumpkin pie spice
1 (5-ounce) can evaporated milk
1 (16-ounce) can pumpkin
1 (2-layer) package yellow butter
  cake mix
1 cup chopped pecans
1 cup (2 sticks) butter, melted

method

Mix the eggs, sugar, cinnamon, nutmeg, pumpkin pie spice, evaporated milk and pumpkin in the order listed in a bowl until smooth. Spoon the batter into a greased 9×13-inch cake pan. Sprinkle with the cake mix and then with the pecans. Drizzle with the butter and bake at 350 degrees for 50 to 60 minutes or until a knife inserted in the center comes out clean. Cool in the pan on a wire rack.

CHOCOLATE SHEET CAKE

Serves 24

ingredients

CAKE

2 cups sugar

2 cups all-purpose flour

1 teaspoon baking soda

1/2 teaspoon salt

1 cup sour cream

2 eggs, lightly beaten

1 cup (2 sticks) butter

1 cup water

1/4 cup baking cocoa

FUDGE FROSTING

1/2 cup (1 stick) butter

1/3 cup milk

1/4 cup baking cocoa

1 (1-pound) package
   confectioners' sugar

1 teaspoon vanilla extract

method

CAKE

Combine the sugar, flour, baking soda and salt in a bowl and mix well. Stir in the sour cream and eggs. Melt the butter in a heavy saucepan over medium heat and whisk in the water and baking cocoa. Bring to a boil, whisking constantly. Remove from the heat and stir into the flour mixture. Pour the batter into a lightly greased 10×15-inch cake pan. Bake at 325 degrees for 20 to 25 minutes or until a wooden pick inserted in the center comes out clean.

FROSTING

Melt the butter in a saucepan over medium heat and whisk in the milk and baking cocoa. Bring to a boil. Remove from the heat and add the confectioners' sugar gradually, whisking constantly until blended. Stir in the vanilla. Spread the frosting over the warm cake. Let stand until set.

The Chocolate Sheet Cake can be prepared without chocolate for a different twist. Serving both on a dessert buffet makes for a fun checkerboard presentation. Cut the White Sheet Cake and Chocolate Sheet Cake into bite-size squares and alternate the squares on a serving platter. To prepare a White Sheet Cake, omit the baking cocoa and substitute 1 teaspoon almond extract for the vanilla extract. Proceed as directed above. To prepare White Frosting, omit the baking cocoa and substitute 1 teaspoon almond extract for the vanilla extract. Proceed as directed above.

SUPERIOR STEAKHOUSE'S KRISPY KREME
BREAD PUDDING

Serves 4

ingredients

12 Krispy Kreme doughnuts
1/2 cup raisins
1 cup sugar
4 eggs, lightly beaten
1 1/2 teaspoons banana flavoring
2 cups heavy cream
Cinnamon-sugar to taste

method

Cut the doughnuts into quarters and arrange in a baking dish sprayed with nonstick cooking spray. Sprinkle with the raisins.

Mix the sugar, eggs and flavoring in a bowl. Bring the heavy cream almost to a boil in a saucepan and add to the egg mixture gradually, whisking constantly. Pour the cream mixture over the doughnuts and sprinkle with cinnamon-sugar. Bake, covered, at 325 degrees for 30 minutes. Remove the cover and bake for 10 minutes longer.

The original Krispy Kreme doughnut recipe came from a chef in New Orleans. In 1937, Vernon Randolph moved to Winston-Salem, North Carolina, with the secret recipe in hand and rented a building in which he started making doughnuts. The rest is history.

NOVEMBER

Who can think about November without being

thankful for Thanksgiving, a holiday that is all

thanksgiving

about family, food, and more food? After your

debutante ball

family's feast, you can enjoy the view from your

sportsman's paradise

recliner or get out and enjoy the scenery of the

sportsman's paradise.

Few people think of November without thinking of Thanksgiving, and the people of Northwest Louisiana, with much to be thankful for, are no different. This day of thanks was celebrated inconsistently for many years until 1941, when Congress finally sanctioned the fourth Thursday in November as the legal holiday. Unlike many holidays, when you traditionally venture out to celebrate, THANKSGIVING is most commonly celebrated at home, in the company of family and friends. Chances are you will celebrate in this way also.

Many begin the day by watching the Macy's Thanksgiving Day Parade, a consistently spectacular celebration known for its policy of going on rain or shine. It was started in the 1920s by department store employees and has been a U.S. Thanksgiving tradition ever since. After Thanksgiving dinner with loved ones, it's time for the sports fans in the house to retire to the comfort of a favorite chair to watch a game of professional or collegiate football. The Detroit Lions have played on this day nearly every year since 1934, and the nearby Dallas Cowboys, a local favorite team for many, have hosted a game on Thanksgiving nearly every year since 1966. Many college football teams also play on Thanksgiving Day, giving the football fan in your family ample opportunity to enjoy the afternoon.

Northwest Louisiana is known as the SPORTSMAN'S PARADISE, and besides athletic events, many people enjoy other outdoor activities in the region this time of year. Thick, piney woods full of wildlife; lush, autumn landscapes full of color; and clear, sparkling lakes full of fish define Northwest Louisiana as a haven for birdwatchers, nature photographers, campers, fishermen, and hunters of all ages. Native Americans trapped deer and traded pottery in the region long before ancient Greece and Rome were even on the map, and this area continues to reward our people with the treasures of nature.

For a more elegant celebration this month, the Shreveport Country Club plays host each November to the Shreveport Demoiselle Club's annual gala. THE DEBUTANTE BALL is a grand finale for college debutantes to make their formal bows to society after a season of parties beginning in June. After the debutantes gracefully promenade around the ballroom on the arms of their chosen escorts, guests dine, dance, and mingle at the truly grand occasion.

Whether you're already home, coming home to visit, or just passing through, November is a special time of year to be in Northwest Louisiana for family, food, and relaxation.

WHITE RUSSIAN

*For a **Black Russian,** omit the milk or cream.*

Serves 1

ingredients

1 part Kahlúa
1 part vodka
1 part milk or cream
Crushed ice

method

Mix the Kahlúa, vodka and milk in a small pitcher and pour over crushed ice in a glass. For a frozen White Russian, blend the Kahlúa mixture with ice in a blender. Substitute raspberry or vanilla vodka for a different flavor.

COCKTAIL CHEESY PUFFS

Serves 12 to 14

ingredients

1 loaf unsliced bread
1 cup (2 sticks) butter or margarine
6 ounces cream cheese, softened
1/2 cup (2 ounces) shredded sharp
   Cheddar cheese
1/2 cup (2 ounces) shredded
   mozzarella cheese
1/2 cup (2 ounces) shredded
   Swiss cheese
1 teaspoon pepper
1/2 teaspoon salt
4 egg whites, stiffly beaten

method

Trim the crusts from the bread and cut the bread into 1-inch cubes. Melt the butter in a saucepan and stir in the cream cheese, Cheddar cheese, mozzarella cheese, Swiss cheese, pepper and salt. Cook until blended, stirring frequently. Fold in the egg whites and remove from the heat.

Coat the bread cubes with the cheese mixture and arrange the coated cubes in a single layer on a baking sheet; do not allow the bread cubes to touch. Freeze until firm and store in sealable freezer bags until needed. Just before serving, arrange the frozen puffs on a baking sheet and bake at 400 degrees for 10 minutes. Serve hot.

CRANBERRY JEZEBEL SAUCE

Serves 32

ingredients

1 cup water
1/2 cup granulated sugar
1/2 cup packed brown sugar
1 (12-ounce) package fresh or
    frozen cranberries
1/2 cup pineapple preserves
3 tablespoons prepared horseradish
1 tablespoon Dijon mustard
16 ounces block-style cream
    cheese

method

Bring the water, granulated sugar and brown sugar to a boil in a saucepan over medium-high heat, stirring frequently. Stir in the cranberries and return to a boil. Reduce the heat to low.

Simmer for 10 minutes or until the cranberries begin to pop and the mixture begins to thicken, stirring frequently. Remove from the heat. Add the preserves, prepared horseradish and Dijon mustard and mix well. Let stand until cool and chill, covered, in the refrigerator. Spoon the chilled cranberry mixture over the cream cheese on a serving platter and serve with assorted party crackers. Serve alongside pork tenderloin or leftover turkey for cocktail sandwiches.

Cranberries will not handle a great amount of heat before the water inside produces enough steam to burst the berry. When cranberries pop and burst, it is time to stop the cooking process; otherwise, the cranberries will become bitter and very tart.

CRANBERRY SALSA*

Makes 2 cups

ingredients

1 (12-ounce) package fresh
   cranberries
4 or 5 green onions, chopped
1 jalapeño chile, seeded
   and chopped
1/2 cup sugar
Grated zest and juice of 2 limes
1/4 teaspoon salt

*Photograph for this recipe on page 173.

method

Place the cranberries in a food processor and pulse until coarsely chopped. Add the green onions and jalapeño chile and pulse several more times. Add the sugar, lime zest, lime juice and salt and pulse until combined. Chill, covered, for 24 hours to enhance the flavor. Serve with tortilla chips.

MARINATED ARTICHOKE SALAD

Serves 8 to 10

ingredients

MARINATED ARTICHOKES
1 cup extra-light virgin olive oil
6 tablespoons grated
   Parmesan cheese
1/4 cup red wine vinegar
1/4 cup lemon juice
2 tablespoons drained finely
   chopped pimento
2 tablespoons sugar
1 tablespoon garlic powder
2 teaspoons salt
1/2 teaspoon pepper
2 (14-ounce) cans artichoke hearts,
   drained and quartered

SALAD
1 head green leaf lettuce, trimmed
   and torn into bite-size pieces
1 head red leaf lettuce, trimmed and
   torn into bite-size pieces
1 purple onion, chopped
1 cup chopped tomato
Croutons

method

ARTICHOKES

Whisk the olive oil, cheese, vinegar, lemon juice, pimento, sugar, garlic powder, salt and pepper in a bowl until combined. Add the artichokes and stir until coated. Marinate, covered, in the refrigerator for 8 to 10 hours, stirring occasionally.

SALAD

Toss the green leaf lettuce, red leaf lettuce, onion and tomato in a large salad bowl. Add the undrained artichokes and toss to combine. Sprinkle with croutons and serve immediately.

GREEN BEAN CASSEROLE

Serves 6 to 8

ingredients

1 (16-ounce) can French-style green
 beans, drained
1 (16-ounce) can white Shoe Peg
 corn, drained
1 (10-ounce) can cream of
 celery soup
1/2 cup sour cream
1/2 cup (2 ounces) shredded sharp
 Cheddar cheese
1/2 cup finely chopped onion
1/8 teaspoon salt
1 sleeve butter crackers, crushed
1/2 cup slivered almonds

method

Layer the green beans and corn in a greased 9×13-inch baking dish. Mix the soup, sour cream, cheese, onion and salt in a bowl and spread over the prepared layers. Sprinkle with the cracker crumbs and almonds and bake at 350 degrees for 45 minutes.

CAULIFLOWER AU GRATIN*

Serves 6

ingredients

Florets of 1 large head cauliflower
2 tablespoons butter
1 onion, finely chopped
3 tablespoons all-purpose flour
2 cups milk
5 ounces blue cheese, crumbled
1/2 teaspoon celery salt
Cayenne pepper to taste
Salt and black pepper to taste
3/4 cup chopped walnuts

*Photograph for this recipe on page 173.

method

Cook the cauliflower in boiling water in a saucepan for 6 minutes or until tender. Drain and arrange the cauliflower in an 8×8-inch baking dish. Melt the butter in a saucepan and add the onion. Sauté until tender and remove from the heat. Add the flour and mix until combined. Add the milk gradually, stirring constantly. Stir in the cheese, celery salt, cayenne pepper, salt and black pepper. Cook until thickened, stirring constantly.

Pour the cheese sauce over the cauliflower and sprinkle with the walnuts. Broil until the walnuts are brown. Serve immediately.

CRANBERRY AND SWEET POTATO BAKE

Serves 4 to 6

ingredients

2 (15-ounce) cans sweet
   potatoes, drained
1 (8-ounce) can crushed
   pineapple, drained
1 egg, lightly beaten
2 tablespoons butter, melted
1/4 teaspoon salt
1/8 teaspoon pepper
1 (16-ounce) can whole
   cranberry sauce

method

Combine the sweet potatoes and pineapple in a large bowl and mash with a potato masher to the desired consistency. Stir in the egg, butter, salt and pepper and swirl in the cranberry sauce. Spoon the cranberry mixture into a 1-quart baking dish and bake at 350 degrees for 40 minutes. Serve immediately.

SUPERIOR STEAKHOUSE'S WHIPPED SWEET POTATOES*

Serves 4

ingredients

8 sweet potatoes
1 cup heavy cream
1/2 cup (1 stick) butter
2 cups maple syrup
1 cup packed brown sugar
1/2 cup granulated sugar
Juice of 2 oranges
1 tablespoon vanilla extract
1 tablespoon ground cinnamon
1 1/2 teaspoons ground nutmeg
Marshmallows (optional)

*Photograph for this recipe on page 173.

method

Arrange the sweet potatoes on a baking sheet and bake at 400 degrees for 1 hour or until tender. Cool slightly and peel the sweet potatoes. Place the pulp in a large bowl.

Heat the heavy cream and butter in a saucepan until the butter melts. Add the butter mixture, maple syrup, brown sugar, granulated sugar, orange juice, vanilla, cinnamon and nutmeg to the sweet potato pulp and whip with an electric mixer until blended and fluffy. Spoon into a baking dish and top with marshmallows. Broil until the marshmallows are brown.

SOUTHERN CORN BREAD DRESSING AND GRAVY

Serves 8 to 10

ingredients

CORN BREAD DRESSING

1 package yellow corn bread mix
   (do not use Jiffy mix)
1 cup finely chopped onion
1 cup finely chopped celery
1 cup herb-seasoned stuffing mix
6 slices white bread, crusts trimmed
   and bread torn
Salt and pepper to taste
4 (14-ounce) cans chicken broth
3 eggs
Milk

SOUTHERN GRAVY

1/4 cup (1/2 stick) butter
All-purpose flour
1/2 (14-ounce) can chicken broth
3 hard-cooked eggs, chopped

method

DRESSING

Prepare and bake the corn bread using the package directions. Cook the onion and celery in a small amount of water in a saucepan for 45 minutes or until tender. Crumble the corn bread into a large bowl and stir in the undrained onion mixture. Add the stuffing mix, white bread, salt and pepper and mix well. Stir in the broth until moistened. The flavor of the dressing is enhanced if chilled for 8 to 10 hours at this point.

Whisk the eggs and a small amount of milk in a bowl until blended. Stir the egg mixture into the corn bread mixture and spoon into a 9×13-inch baking dish. Bake at 375 degrees for 1 hour or until brown and crisp around the edges.

GRAVY

Melt the butter in a skillet and stir in a small amount of flour until blended. Cook until bubbly and mix in the broth. Stir in the eggs and cook until thickened, stirring frequently and adding additional broth as needed. Serve with the dressing.

*I*n 1985, our largest coalition ever resulted in The LightHouse, a beacon of hope for children and teenagers striving to overcome poverty, illiteracy, and joblessness in Shreveport's Ledbetter Heights neighborhood. Now a part of Volunteers of America, it has since spread to five other locations, which maintain the same program and standards. The LightHouse tracks the attendance and school grades, provides discipline, coordinates extracurricular activities, and manages encounters with juvenile court for all the program's children.

GRILLED TENDERLOIN WITH BLUEBERRY SAUCE*

Serves 12 to 15

ingredients

TENDERLOINS
3 venison, beef or pork tenderloins
1 cup vegetable oil
3/4 cup soy sauce
1/2 cup red wine vinegar
1/3 cup fresh lemon juice
1/4 cup Worcestershire sauce
2 tablespoons dry mustard
2 tablespoons chopped fresh parsley
1 tablespoon freshly ground pepper
2 teaspoons salt
2 garlic cloves, crushed

BLUEBERRY BARBECUE SAUCE
1 tablespoon olive oil
1/4 cup minced onion
1 tablespoon chopped fresh
   jalapeño chile
1 pint fresh blueberries
3 tablespoons brown sugar
1/4 cup rice vinegar
1/4 cup ketchup
3 tablespoons Dijon mustard
1 teaspoon Tabasco sauce
1/4 cup (1/2 stick) unsalted butter
Salt and pepper to taste

*Photograph for this recipe on page 173.

method

TENDERLOINS
Arrange the tenderloins in a shallow dish. Whisk the oil, soy sauce, vinegar, lemon juice, Worcestershire sauce, dry mustard, parsley, pepper, salt and garlic in a bowl and pour over the tenderloins, turning to coat. Marinate, covered, in the refrigerator for 4 to 5 hours, turning occasionally; drain.

Grill the venison tenderloins over medium-hot coals for 14 to 15 minutes, turning once. If using beef tenderloins, grill for at least 30 minutes. Remove the tenderloins to a serving platter and slice as desired.

SAUCE
Heat the olive oil in a large skillet and add the onion and jalapeño chile. Sauté until the onion is tender and stir in the blueberries, brown sugar, vinegar, ketchup, Dijon mustard and Tabasco sauce. Bring to a low boil and cook for 15 minutes, stirring constantly.

Pour the blueberry mixture into a blender and process until puréed. Strain the purée into a small saucepan, discarding the solids. Cook until heated through, stirring frequently. Stir in the butter and cook until blended. Season with salt and pepper and serve immediately with the tenderloins. You may prepare the sauce in advance, adding the butter just before serving.

VENISON CHILI

Makes 7 cups

ingredients

1¹/₂ to 2 pounds ground venison or
 lean ground beef
1 large onion, finely chopped (1 cup)
1 teaspoon salt
¹/₂ cup (or more) all-purpose flour
1 (46-ounce) can tomato juice
1 (10-ounce) can tomatoes with
 green chiles
1 envelope chili mix

method

Sauté the venison in a skillet until no longer pink and drain. Add the onion and cook until the onion is tender but not brown, stirring frequently. Stir in the salt. Brown the flour in a dry skillet; do not burn. Bring the tomato juice to a boil in a stockpot and stir in the undrained tomatoes.

Mix the browned flour with the venison mixture and stir into the tomato juice mixture. Add the chili mix and mix well. Simmer for 30 minutes and ladle into chili bowls. You may add 1 can of ranch-style beans to the chili or serve the beans with the chili.

ORANGE HONEY-GLAZED CORNISH GAME HENS*

Serves 4

ingredients

2 (1¹/₄-pound) Cornish game hens,
 split into halves
¹/₄ cup orange juice
2 tablespoons soy sauce
1 tablespoon white wine vinegar
1 teaspoon honey
¹/₈ teaspoon ground ginger

*Photograph for this recipe on page 173.

method

Arrange the hens cut side down in a roasting pan and roast at 400 degrees for 30 minutes. Whisk the orange juice, soy sauce, vinegar, honey and ginger in a bowl until blended.

Brush the orange juice mixture over the hens and roast for 10 minutes longer or until the juices run clear when the hens are pricked with a fork and the skin is brown and crisp.

DUCK GUMBO

Serves 8 to 12

ingredients

3 ribs celery, chopped

2 green onions, chopped

1 yellow onion, chopped

1 bell pepper, chopped

1 (16-ounce) package frozen okra

Butter

2 to 2½ quarts water

1 package Louisiana Fish Fry
  gumbo mix

2 large ducks or chickens,
  smoked, boned and cut into
  bite-size pieces

8 to 16 ounces spicy smoked
  sausage, cut into bite-size pieces

1 (16-ounce) can Italian stewed
  tomatoes

2 tablespoons (or more)
  Tabasco sauce

1 teaspoon filé powder

1 teaspoon garlic salt

½ to 1 teaspoon red pepper

Black pepper to taste

1 pint oysters, or peeled
  cooked shrimp

Hot cooked rice

method

Sauté the celery, green onions, yellow onion, bell pepper and okra in butter in a stockpot until the vegetables are tender. Add the water, gumbo mix, duck, sausage, undrained tomatoes, Tabasco sauce, filé powder, garlic salt, red pepper and black pepper to the sautéed vegetables and mix well.

Simmer for 1½ hours, stirring occasionally. Add the undrained oysters 20 minutes before the end of the cooking process and mix well. Ladle over hot cooked rice in bowls.

Keep **Cream Biscuits** in the freezer for hot biscuits any time. Mix 1½ cups self-rising flour and 1 cup heavy cream in a bowl until a smooth dough forms. Roll ½ inch thick on a lightly floured surface and cut into rounds with a small cutter. Arrange the rounds 1 inch apart on a baking sheet. Bake at 425 degrees for 10 minutes or until golden brown. Serve immediately or freeze on a baking sheet for future use. Store the frozen biscuits in sealable freezer bags. Makes 3 dozen biscuits.

Photograph for this recipe on page 173.

WALKER'S DUCKS

Serves 6

6 teal or other small ducks, or
   the equivalent in larger
   ducks, dressed
All-purpose flour for coating
Salt and freshly ground black
   pepper to taste
1/2 to 3/4 cup olive oil
1/2 cup (1 stick) unsalted butter
2 white onions, chopped
2 tablespoons all-purpose flour
2 cups ham stock
1/4 cup madeira or marsala
1/4 cup dry sherry
1 small can apple juice
3/4 cup orange juice
1/4 teaspoon cayenne pepper
1/4 cup soy sauce
3 bay leaves
1/2 teaspoon salt
1/4 teaspoon black pepper
Hot cooked wild rice or brown rice

Coat the ducks with a mixture of flour and salt and black pepper to taste. Heat the olive oil in a Dutch oven until very hot and arrange the ducks breast side down in the hot oil. Cook for 10 minutes or until brown on all sides, turning once. Remove the ducks to a platter and discard most of the pan drippings.

Heat the butter with the remaining reserved pan drippings over medium heat and stir in the onions and 2 tablespoons flour. Sauté until the onions begin to brown and a nut-brown roux forms. Stir in the ham stock, wine, sherry, apple juice and orange juice and bring to a simmer over medium heat. Return the ducks to the Dutch oven; at least 60 percent of the surface of the ducks should be covered by the wine mixture. Stir in the cayenne pepper, soy sauce, bay leaves, 1/2 teaspoon salt and 1/4 teaspoon black pepper.

Simmer over low heat until thickened, stirring occasionally. Cover and continue cooking for 2 1/2 to 3 hours or until the meat begins to separate from the bones. Discard the bay leaves and ladle over hot cooked wild rice or brown rice. Serve with a red wine such as merlot, cabernet or pinot noir. You can brown quail in olive oil, lightly coat with flour and add to the Dutch oven about 1 hour before removing the ducks, if desired.

NOTE: *Ham stock is available in the gourmet section of most supermarkets. It comes in a concentrated form and stores well in the refrigerator. Reconstitute by adding water and heating in the microwave for several minutes.*

CRANBERRY RAISIN BREAD PUDDING

Serves 4 to 6

ingredients

BREAD PUDDING

3/4 cup half-and-half

1/2 cup sugar

1/2 cup (1 stick) butter, melted

2 eggs, beaten

1 (16-ounce) loaf raisin bread, cubed

1/2 to 1 cup fresh or frozen cranberries

LEMON VANILLA SAUCE

1/2 cup sugar

2 tablespoons cornstarch

1/8 teaspoon salt

1 cup water

1 teaspoon vanilla extract

1 tablespoon butter

1/3 cup fresh lemon juice (2 large lemons)

2 tablespoons grated lemon zest

method

BREAD PUDDING

Combine the half-and-half, sugar, butter and eggs in a bowl and mix well. Fold in the bread cubes and cranberries. Spoon the pudding mixture into a lightly greased 8×8-inch baking pan and bake at 350 degrees for 25 minutes.

SAUCE

Mix the sugar, cornstarch and salt in a saucepan. Stir in the water and vanilla. Cook over medium heat until thickened and smooth, stirring constantly. Stir in the butter, lemon juice and lemon zest. Cook just until heated through, stirring frequently. Serve warm with the bread pudding.

The Junior League began a new project in 1995 at the Providence House, a residential development center for homeless families with children. League members assist in breaking the cycle of homelessness by offering activities for children that raise self-esteem, teach age-appropriate life skills, explore creative expression through art, and reinforce basic lessons learned in school. Comprehensive support services are provided for improving the family structure and moving the family into independent living.

STREUSEL-TOPPED PUMPKIN PIE*

Serves 8

ingredients

PUMPKIN PIE

1¼ cups cold milk

1 cup canned pumpkin

2 (4-ounce) packages cheesecake
  instant pudding mix

1 teaspoon pumpkin pie spice

4 ounces whipped topping

1 (9-inch) graham cracker pie shell

**STREUSEL TOPPING AND
  ASSEMBLY**

½ cup chopped walnuts

1 tablespoon butter

2 teaspoons brown sugar

4 ounces whipped topping

*Photograph for this recipe on page 173.

method

PIE

Mix the milk and pumpkin in a bowl until smooth. Add the pudding mix and pumpkin pie spice and whisk until blended. Stir in the whipped topping. Spoon into the pie shell and chill, covered, for 4 hours or until set.

TOPPING

Combine the walnuts, butter and brown sugar in a microwave-safe bowl and microwave on High for 2½ minutes, stirring once. Let stand until cool. Sprinkle the streusel over the top of the pie and spread with the whipped topping just before serving. Decrease the fat grams by using skim milk and fat-free whipped topping.

CARAMEL CHOCOLATE SQUARES

Makes 2 to 3 dozen squares

ingredients

1 (14-ounce) package light caramels

⅓ cup evaporated milk

1 (2-layer) package German
  chocolate cake mix

¾ cup (1½ sticks) margarine,
  melted and cooled

⅓ cup evaporated milk

1 cup pecans, chopped (optional)

1 cup (6 ounces) semisweet
  chocolate chips

method

Combine the caramels and ⅓ cup evaporated milk in a heavy saucepan. Cook over low heat until blended, stirring constantly. Combine the cake mix, margarine, ⅓ cup evaporated milk and the pecans in a bowl and mix well. Press one-half of the cake mix mixture over the bottom of a greased and floured 9×13-inch baking pan and bake at 350 degrees for 6 minutes. Spread the caramel mixture over the baked layer and sprinkle with the chocolate chips. Crumble the remaining cake mix mixture over the top and bake for 15 to 18 minutes longer or until the edges pull from the sides of the pan. Cool in the pan on a wire rack and cut into squares.

SOFT GINGERSNAPS

Makes 5 dozen cookies

ingredients

4 cups all-purpose flour
4 teaspoons baking soda
1 tablespoon ground ginger
2 teaspoons ground cinnamon
1 teaspoon salt
2 cups sugar
1½ cups canola oil
½ cup molasses
2 eggs
Sugar for coating

method

Sift the flour, baking soda, ginger, cinnamon and salt into a bowl and mix well. Combine 2 cups sugar, the canola oil, molasses and eggs in a large mixing bowl and beat until blended. Stir in the flour mixture and chill, covered, for 1 hour.

Shape the dough by teaspoonfuls into balls and coat with sugar. Arrange the coated balls on an ungreased cookie sheet and bake at 350 degrees for 6 to 8 minutes; do not overbake. Cool on the cookie sheet for 2 minutes and remove to a wire rack to cool completely. The cookies are done if they are puffy and cracked. They will flatten as they cool. Store in an airtight container.

Good-quality fresh ginger should have smooth, light brown skin with a light sheen and white flesh. Pick the roots with the fewest knots and/or branching and store in the refrigerator. Fresh ginger may be frozen for up to three months.

DECEMBER

Whether you are celebrating Christmas,

Hanukkah, Kwanzaa, or some other holiday,

festival of lights

December is a time of the year filled with the

christmas in roseland

spirit of generosity and festive gatherings of

rockets over the red

family, friends, and loved ones.

independence bowl

ecember marks the official beginning of winter and the end of the year. Most often, however, when you think of December, you think of Christmas. The spirit of Christmas, generosity and goodwill toward others, is also found in the celebrations of most other religions. So whether you celebrate CHRISTMAS, HANUKKAH, KWANZAA, or some other holiday in December, you're bound to be touched with warmth and good cheer.

Many festivals are found around the country to help usher in the official holiday season, and we have our fair share. Few celebrations get area residents into the Christmas spirit like the FESTIVAL OF LIGHTS in Natchitoches. This well-known festival is one of the nation's oldest community-based holiday celebrations. Beginning two days before Thanksgiving, festival goers can experience the charm of the oldest French colony in Louisiana. The city of Natchitoches is transformed into the "City of Lights," with more than 350,000 lights and over 200,000 visitors. A spectacular fireworks show over the scenic Cane River Lake kicks off the festival, which lasts through December and into January.

This begins the Holiday Trail of Lights, a festive collaboration of light displays in cities throughout Northwest Louisiana and East Texas. Shreveport and Bossier City celebrate the splendor of Christmas all month with DECEMBER ON THE RED, a holiday lighting spectacular, and ROCKETS OVER THE RED, which ushers in the season with music, games, tasty delicacies, Santa's arrival by train, and a fireworks show held the weekend after Thanksgiving. The American Rose Center is also transformed into a world of lights each year. Its CHRISTMAS IN ROSELAND offers a fantasy wonderland of lights, holiday scenes, and nightly entertainment beginning the day after Thanksgiving and lasting throughout the Christmas season. To prove that smaller can be better, the CLAIBORNE CHRISTMAS FESTIVAL, held the weekend after Thanksgiving in Homer, promises a full day of fun and Christmas spirit for the entire family.

A creative twist on the season can be found at the Antique Car Museum in Shreveport, which hosts the annual FESTIVAL OF TREES. The first festival was the creation of the parents club of St. Mark's Day School in the early 1980s. Now hosted by the museum, the festival gives you a glimpse of life during Charles Dickens's time, and many beautiful and uniquely decorated Christmas trees are scattered among the vintage cars.

Bring the year to a close by heading to Shreveport for the INDEPENDENCE BOWL, the last bowl game of the year. Its name can be traced back to the first game held on December 13, 1976, chosen to honor the United States' 200th birthday and the men and women who have fought for our freedom and independence. It has been Northwest Louisiana's own contribution to post-season collegiate football ever since.

Nowadays, many people are back into their normal routines before the mistletoe is even wilted, but don't forget that the holiday season actually lasts until January 6th, which means the Twelfth Night celebration kicking off Mardi Gras is just around the corner!

CINNAMON WINTER CIDER

Makes about 13 cups

ingredients

1 (12-ounce) can frozen apple juice
  concentrate, thawed
1 (12-ounce) can frozen cranberry
  juice concentrate, thawed
1 (6-ounce) can frozen lemonade
  concentrate, thawed
9 cups water
5 cinnamon sticks
6 whole cloves
1 teaspoon ground nutmeg
1/3 cup cinnamon schnapps (optional)

method

Mix the apple juice concentrate, cranberry juice concentrate, lemonade concentrate, water, cinnamon sticks, cloves and nutmeg in a Dutch oven and bring to a boil. Reduce the heat to low.

Simmer, covered, for 15 minutes. Remove from the heat and discard the cinnamon sticks and cloves. Stir in the schnapps and serve warm in mugs. You may freeze the cider in 1-cup servings before adding the schnapps. Thaw and reheat, adding 1 to 1 1/2 tablespoons schnapps per cup.

PEPPERMINT PUNCH

Peppermint ice cream is sold only during the holidays.
Serves 16

ingredients

1 pint peppermint ice cream
2 cups dairy eggnog
1 (12-ounce) can club soda, chilled
Red food coloring
1 cup heavy whipping
  cream, whipped
1/3 cup crushed peppermint candy
16 peppermint sticks

method

Place the ice cream in a chilled punch bowl. Stir in the eggnog and club soda. Tint as desired with red food coloring. Spread the whipped cream over the surface of the punch and sprinkle with the crushed peppermint. Garnish each serving with a peppermint stick.

SUGARED CRANBERRIES

. . . .

Makes 3 cups

ingredients

2 cups granulated sugar
2 cups water
1 (12-ounce) package fresh or
  frozen cranberries
Superfine sugar

method

Combine the granulated sugar and water in a small saucepan and cook over low heat until the sugar dissolves, stirring occasionally. Bring to a simmer and remove from the heat; do not boil. Stir in the cranberries and pour into a heatproof bowl. Chill, covered, for 8 to 10 hours.

Drain the cranberries in a colander. Coat the cranberries with superfine sugar and spread in a single layer on a sheet of waxed paper or baking parchment. Let stand for 1 hour or until dry. Store in an airtight container for up to 1 week.

HERBED OYSTER CRACKERS

. . . .

Makes 6 cups

ingredients

1 cup vegetable oil
1 tablespoon dill weed
$1/2$ teaspoon lemon pepper
1 envelope ranch salad
  dressing mix
1 (10-ounce) package
  oyster crackers

method

Combine the oil, dill weed, lemon pepper and salad dressing mix in a bowl and whisk until blended. Pour over the oyster crackers in a bowl and mix to coat well. Store in an airtight container for 24 hours before serving.

WARM ARTICHOKE AND SALSA DIP

. . . .

Serves 4 to 6

ingredients

1 (12-ounce) jar marinated artichoke
  hearts, drained
1/3 cup sliced green onions
2 tablespoons bottled green salsa
1/2 cup (2 ounces) shredded
  Monterey Jack cheese
1/4 cup sour cream
1/4 cup snipped fresh cilantro

method

Coarsely chop the artichokes and combine with the green onions and salsa in a small saucepan. Cook over medium heat until heated through, stirring frequently. Remove from the heat and stir in the cheese, sour cream and cilantro. Serve immediately with chips.

HOT ONION SOUFFLÉ DIP

. . . .

Serves 20 to 25

ingredients

2 cups finely chopped Vidalia
  onions or other sweet onions
16 ounces cream cheese, softened
2 cups (8 ounces) grated
  Parmesan cheese
1/2 cup mayonnaise
Paprika to taste

method

Combine the onions, cream cheese, Parmesan cheese and mayonnaise in a bowl and mix well. Spoon the onion mixture into an 8×8-inch baking pan and sprinkle with paprika. Bake at 350 degrees for 20 to 30 minutes or until heated through. Serve hot with assorted party crackers and/or party bread.

BROWN RICE CHICKEN CRANBERRY SALAD

Serves 6 to 8

ingredients

4 cups cooked brown rice
2 cups chopped cooked
 chicken breasts
1 cup dried cranberries, chopped
1 cup grape halves
1 bunch scallions, trimmed and
 chopped (about 4)
1/2 cup slivered almonds, toasted
1 tablespoon chopped fresh
 thyme leaves
1 cup mayonnaise
1/4 cup honey
1/4 cup Dijon mustard
2 tablespoons balsamic vinegar
Salt and pepper to taste

method

Combine the brown rice, chicken, cranberries, grapes, scallions, almonds and thyme in a bowl and mix well. Combine the mayonnaise, honey, Dijon mustard, vinegar, salt and pepper in a bowl and whisk until thickened. Add the mayonnaise mixture to the rice mixture and toss to coat. Chill, covered, until serving time.

GREEN BEAN BUNDLES

Serves 6 to 8

ingredients

8 ounces sliced bacon
2 (14-ounce) cans whole green
 beans, drained
Garlic salt to taste
6 tablespoons butter
1/2 cup packed light brown sugar

method

Cut each slice of bacon into thirds. Bundle 6 to 8 green beans and wrap with a piece of bacon. Secure with a wooden pick and arrange the bundle in a 1 1/2-quart baking dish. Repeat the process with the remaining green beans and bacon. Sprinkle with garlic salt.

Melt the butter in a small saucepan and stir in the brown sugar. Cook for 1 minute or until the brown sugar melts, stirring frequently. Pour the brown sugar mixture over the green beans and bake at 325 degrees for 30 to 40 minutes or until the bacon is brown and cooked through.

BAKED POTATO CASSEROLE

• •

Serves 6 to 8

ingredients

5 or 6 large baking potatoes, peeled
   and coarsely chopped
1/2 cup (1 stick) butter, softened
Salt and pepper to taste
8 ounces cream cheese, softened
1 cup sour cream
2 cups (8 ounces) shredded
   Cheddar cheese
Chopped green onions
Bacon bits

method

Combine the potatoes with enough water to generously cover in a saucepan and bring to a boil. Boil until the potatoes are fork-tender and drain. Mash the potatoes, butter, salt and pepper in a bowl. Add the cream cheese and sour cream and mix well.

Spoon the potato mixture into a 9×13-inch baking pan and sprinkle with the Cheddar cheese. Bake at 350 degrees for 30 minutes or until brown and bubbly. Sprinkle with green onions and bacon bits. You may prepare the casserole in advance and store, covered, in the refrigerator. Bake just before serving. You can prepare **Twice-Baked Potatoes** by baking the potatoes, mixing the potato pulp with the remaining ingredients and stuffing the potato mixture into the potato shells. Bake as directed above.

*I*n 2004, the Junior League began providing another fantastic and life-changing community project, Paired Reading at Atkins Elementary. League members mentor first grade students to help them develop a lifelong love of reading. Each week as League members meet with these students, the students' lives are changed and forever enriched.

CORN BREAD CASSEROLE

Serves 4 to 6

ingredients

1 (16-ounce) can whole kernel corn, drained
1 (17-ounce) can cream-style corn
1 package corn muffin mix
1 egg, lightly beaten
2 tablespoons butter, melted
1/2 teaspoon sugar

method

Combine the corn, muffin mix, egg, butter and sugar in a bowl and mix well. Spoon the corn mixture into a 7×11-inch or 8×8-inch baking dish and bake at 400 degrees for 25 to 30 minutes or until light golden brown.

CHICKEN SPAGHETTI

Serves 6

ingredients

3 pounds chicken pieces
8 ounces spaghetti, broken
1/4 cup (1/2 stick) butter
1/4 cup all-purpose flour
1 cup half-and-half
1 cup chicken broth
1 cup mayonnaise
1 cup sour cream
3/4 cup (3 ounces) grated Parmesan cheese
1/3 cup white wine
2 tablespoons lemon juice
1 teaspoon dry mustard
1 teaspoon salt
1/2 teaspoon garlic powder
8 ounces fresh mushrooms, sliced
1/4 cup (1 ounce) grated Parmesan cheese
Paprika to taste

method

Combine the chicken with enough water to generously cover in a Dutch oven and bring to a boil. Boil until tender. Remove the chicken to a platter using a slotted spoon, reserving the stock. Bring the reserved stock to a boil and add the pasta. Cook until the pasta is tender and drain. Chop the chicken, discarding the skin and bones.

Melt the butter in a large saucepan and stir in the flour. Cook until bubbly, stirring constantly. Add the half-and-half and broth and mix well. Cook until thickened, stirring constantly. Stir in the mayonnaise, sour cream, Parmesan cheese, wine, lemon juice, dry mustard, salt and garlic powder. Remove from the heat.

Sauté the mushrooms in a nonstick skillet until tender. Mix the mushrooms, pasta and chicken in a bowl and spoon into a 3-quart baking dish. Bake, covered, at 350 degrees for 25 minutes. Uncover and sprinkle with 1/4 cup cheese and paprika and bake for 10 minutes longer.

BEEF TENDERLOIN WITH MUSHROOMS

Serves 12 to 15

ingredients

1/4 cup (1/2 stick) margarine
1 pound fresh mushrooms, sliced
1 cup chopped green onions
1/4 cup chopped fresh parsley
1 (6- to 7-pound) beef tenderloin
1/2 teaspoon seasoned salt
1/4 teaspoon lemon pepper
1 (8-ounce) bottle red wine vinegar
    and oil salad dressing
Crushed peppercorns

method

Melt the margarine in a skillet and add the mushrooms and green onions. Sauté until tender and drain. Stir in the parsley. Trim the excess fat from the tenderloin. Cut the tenderloin lengthwise into halves to within 1/2 inch of the other edge, leaving one long side connected. Sprinkle the surface of the tenderloin with seasoned salt and lemon pepper.

Spread the mushroom mixture over the cut side and fold over to enclose the filling. Tie securely at 2-inch intervals with kitchen twine. Place the tenderloin in a large sealable plastic bag and pour the salad dressing over the tenderloin; seal tightly. Marinate in the refrigerator for 8 hours or longer, turning occasionally; drain. Press the peppercorns all over the outside of the tenderloin.

Grill, covered or tented with foil, over medium-hot coals for 35 minutes or until a meat thermometer registers 140 degrees for rare or 160 degrees for medium. Remove the tenderloin to a serving platter, discard the twine and slice as desired. You may bake the roast at 350 degrees for 40 minutes for rare or to the desired degree of doneness.

When a roast is brought to room temperature or near room temperature, it will cook more quickly than one that is placed into the oven directly from the refrigerator. This will also prevent the outside of the roast from overcooking and becoming too dry before the inside is done.

MUSTARD-ROASTED SALMON WITH CRANBERRY SAUCE

Serves 6

ingredients

6 tablespoons Dijon mustard

3 tablespoons unsalted butter, melted

6 (6-ounce) salmon fillets

Salt and pepper to taste

3 tablespoons unsalted butter

6 tablespoons chopped shallots or onions

6 tablespoons cranberry sauce

6 tablespoons raspberry vinegar

method

Combine the Dijon mustard and 3 tablespoons butter in a small bowl and whisk until blended. Place the salmon skin side down on an oiled baking sheet. Season with salt. Spread the mustard mixture over the salmon. Sprinkle generously with pepper. Bake at 450 degrees for 10 minutes or until the salmon is cooked through and the mustard is browned.

Heat the remaining 3 tablespoons butter in a small heavy skillet over medium heat. Add the shallots and sauté for 2 minutes. Add the cranberry sauce and vinegar and stir until the cranberry sauce melts and the mixture is smooth. Bring to a simmer. Spoon over the fish.

CHRISTMAS MORNING EGGS

Serves 6

ingredients

6 thin slices luncheon-style ham

6 eggs

2 tablespoons half-and-half

3 tablespoons shredded mild white cheese or mild Cheddar cheese

method

Coat six muffin cups with nonstick cooking spray. Arrange 1 slice of ham in each prepared muffin cup and top each slice of ham with 1 egg. Drizzle each egg with 1 teaspoon of the half-and-half and sprinkle each with $1^1/2$ teaspoons of the cheese. Bake at 450 degrees for 10 minutes. Carefully remove the eggs to serving plates. Let stand for several minutes to allow the egg yolks to continue hardening. You may omit the ham if serving sausage or bacon.

CHOCOLATE CHIP POUND CAKE

Serves 16

ingredients

1 (2-layer) package yellow butter
   cake mix
1 (6-ounce) package chocolate
   instant pudding mix
1/2 cup vegetable oil
1/2 cup water
4 eggs
1 cup sour cream
1 cup (6 ounces) semisweet
   chocolate chips
Confectioners' sugar

method

Combine the cake mix, pudding mix, oil, water, eggs and sour cream in a mixing bowl and beat for 2 minutes, scraping the bowl occasionally. Stir in the chocolate chips and spoon the batter into a greased and floured 10-inch tube pan or bundt pan. Bake at 350 degrees for 1 hour or until a wooden pick inserted near the center comes out clean. Cool in the pan for 10 minutes and remove to a wire rack to cool completely. Dust with confectioners' sugar.

GRAND CHOCOLATE PIE

Serves 10 to 12

ingredients

1/3 cup semisweet chocolate chips
1 tablespoon butter
1 baked (9-inch) deep-dish pie shell
20 vanilla caramels
1/3 cup heavy whipping cream
1 1/2 cups lightly salted peanuts,
   coarsely chopped
1/2 cup milk
1 1/3 cups semisweet chocolate chips
15 large marshmallows
1/4 teaspoon vanilla extract
1 cup heavy whipping cream
1 jar caramel ice cream topping

method

Combine 1/3 cup chocolate chips and the butter in a heavy saucepan and cook over low heat until blended, stirring constantly. Spread the chocolate mixture over the bottom and side of the pie shell. Chill for 15 minutes or until set. Combine the caramels and 1/3 cup heavy whipping cream in a saucepan and cook over medium heat until blended, stirring constantly. Stir in the peanuts. Spoon the peanut mixture into the pie shell. Chill in the refrigerator. Combine the milk, 1 1/3 cups chocolate chips and the marshmallows in a saucepan and cook over low heat until blended, stirring constantly. Remove from the heat and stir in the vanilla. Let stand until cool. Beat 1 cup heavy whipping cream in a mixing bowl until soft peaks form. Fold the whipped cream into the chocolate mixture. Spread the chocolate mixture over the layers in the pie shell. Chill for 3 hours or until set. Drizzle with the caramel topping.

CANDY CANE SNOWBALLS

Makes 5 dozen cookies

ingredients

2 cups (4 sticks) butter, softened
1 cup confectioners' sugar
1 teaspoon vanilla extract
3 1/2 cups all-purpose flour
1 cup chopped pecans
8 ounces white candy coating, chopped
1/3 to 1/2 cup crushed peppermint candy

method

Beat the butter and confectioners' sugar in a mixing bowl until creamy, scraping the bowl occasionally. Stir in the vanilla. Add the flour gradually, beating constantly until blended. Stir in the pecans. Chill, covered, for 3 to 4 hours or until the dough is easily handled. Shape the dough into 1-inch balls and arrange the balls 2 inches apart on an ungreased cookie sheet. Bake at 350 degrees for 18 to 20 minutes or until light brown. Cool on the cookie sheet for 2 minutes and remove to a wire rack to cool completely. Place the candy coating in a microwave-safe bowl and microwave until smooth, stirring occasionally. Dip the top of each cookie in the candy coating and then in the crushed peppermint candy. Let stand on a wire rack until set.

ANDES CHOCOLATE MINT COOKIES

Makes 4 dozen cookies

ingredients

2 1/2 cups all-purpose flour
1 1/4 tablespoons baking soda
1/2 teaspoon salt
2 cups (12 ounces) chocolate chips
1 1/2 cups sugar
3/4 cup (1 1/2 sticks) margarine
2 tablespoons water
2 eggs, beaten
1 package Andes mints

method

Mix the flour, baking soda and salt together. Combine the chocolate chips, sugar, margarine and water in a microwave-safe bowl and microwave until blended, stirring occasionally. Cool slightly and stir in the eggs. Add the flour mixture and mix well. Chill, covered, for 1 hour. The dough will stiffen. Shape the dough into 1-inch balls and arrange 1 inch apart on a nonstick cookie sheet. Bake at 350 degrees for 12 to 13 minutes. Immediately place 1 mint on each cookie. Swirl with a knife when almost melted. Cool on the cookie sheet for 2 minutes and remove to a wire rack to cool completely.

CONTRIBUTORS AND TESTERS

Susan Adams
Lori Allen
Margaret Allums
Marilyn Anderson
Ruby Anderson
Lisa Andress
Betty Arceneaux
Petra Barber
Steve Barber
Kathy Barlow
Natalie Bartle
Martha Barton
Michelle Basco
Stephanie Bass
Laura Batson
Lolly Bearden
Patsy Bell
Jarvia Belton
Brooke Benson
Bess Black
Betty Black
Joey Black
Jeri Bowen
Cris Bower
Leigh Bowman
Cris Bregman
Wynona Breit
Heather Brossette
Dodie Brown
Lettie Burwell
Beverly Byrd
Pam Byrd
Mickey Carlisle
Kristi Carr
Pam Chaney
Virginia Chastain
Grayson Clarke
Eleanor Colquitt

Julie Colvin
Heather Conly
Carolyn Copeland
Isabelle Chapman Corbett
Neal Cox
Madge Davis
Helen DeBeaux
Kay deBerardinis
Ann Dodson
Melinda Dorsett
Teena Doxey
Karen Eason
Leta Eaves
Amy Evans
Denise Evans
Evelyn Evans
Susan Evans
Lory Ann Evensky
Caroline Fischer
Kim FitzGerald
Mikki Fleniken
Carolyn Ford
JoDett Freeman
Paula Frierson
Minou Fritze
Knox Goodman
Gayle Gordon
Julia Graham
Catherine Gregorio
Laura Gregorio
Marina Gregorio
Vita Gregorio
Joan Gresham
Carolyn Griffen
Martha Griffith
Prissy Grozinger
Nancy Guin
Elba Hamilton

Rebecca Hamilton
Margaret Hargrove
Beth Harrington
Lt. Gen. Edgar Harris, USAF ret.
Mary Catherine Harris
Chelsea Haskew
Beth Hayes
Pat Hendrick
Kathryn Hill
A. J. Hodges
Jennifer Holloway
Rhonda Holloway
Sissy Hooper
Kay Howerton
Alice Ann Hutlas
Heather Hutto
Kay Jarrett
Casie Jefcoat
Harriette Johnson
Rachel Johnson
Tara Johnston
Cindy Jones
Amanda Kairschner
Mary Jo Kayser
Kelly Kent
Elissa Larremore
Monica Lawrence
Allyson Lawson
Agnes LeBleu
Maj. Jason W. LeBleu
Teresa LeBleu
Peggy Liddell
Lona Lockard
Cindy Lott
Margaret Lott
Ginger Lukacs
Gina MaHaffey
Tanya Martinez

Lynn Massad
Rochelle Massad
Judy McCarthy
Johnette McCrery
Betty McDonald
Maggie McElroy
Mary Ellen McGee-Jayroe
Molly McInnis
Jodie McJunkins
Vickie Meadows
Lucy Medvec
Camille Meehan
Michelle Morgan
Dr. Kevin Netterville
Pam O'Brien
Margaret Oden
Carolyn Ogilvie
Michelle Osborn
Ann Osment
Emilie Ann Ostendorff, Jr.
Mary Pabst
Sybil Patten
Cynthia Peatross
Jodi Penn
Angie Phares
Carol Ann Pirtle
Mary Pittman

Connie Posner
Tracy Prestwood
Rosemary Pullen
Evelyn Quinn
Vicki Rachal
Courtney Rayburn
Sharon Reed
Betsy Roberts
Dixey Robertson
Kristen Rockett
Peggy Dean St. Martin
Gloria Sartor
Emily Schaumburg
Sue Scheel
Becky Scott
Leslie Scott
Carolyn Sharpe
Libby Siskron
F. Thomas Siskron IV
Martha Siskron
Shannon Slatton
Ashley Smith
Camy Smith
Holly Smith
Frances Smitherman
Susan Snyder
Missie Soignier

Melanie Sotak
Flip Spooner
Brandon Stephens
Dorothy Stephens
Molly Stewart
Lane Stone
Kim Stroud
Nadean Tanner
Cindy Tarver
Mary Tipton
Farris Todd
Imelda Torres
Josefina Torres
Lisa Travis
Helen Turner
Katherine Tyrrell
Angela Waltman
Frances Washburne
Mary Weston
Kendra Wheeler
Sara Margaret White
Sonya Wilson
Suzanne Wolfe
Linda Yates
Sandy Yates
Barbara Zaffater

PROFESSIONAL CONTRIBUTORS

Bella Fresca
Cambridge Club
Chianti
Fairfield Market
Fairway Gift Garden
Ferrier's Rollin' in the Dough

Fertitta's 6301
Landers Dodge
Lewis Gifts
L'Oasis
Mabry House
Shugualak Farms

Strawn's Eat Shop
Superior Grill
Superior Steakhouse
Suzy Littlejohn of
    Simply Tasteful
    personal chef service

INDEX

Accompaniments. *See also* Salsas; Sauces,
    Savory; Sauces, Sweet
    Cranberry Jezebel Sauce, 175
    Cranberry Pear Relish, 16
    Pico de Gallo, 54
    Sauza Tequila Lime Butter, 88
    Southern Gravy, 179

Appetizers. *See also* Dips; Spreads
    Artichoke Bread, 130
    Asparagus Party Rolls, 15
    Brown Sugar Brie, 142
    Cheezies, 63
    Chianti's Eggplant Rolls in Tomato Sauce, 48
    Chicken Bacon Bites with Apricot Sauce, 94
    Cinnamon-Sugar Crisps, 129
    Cocktail Cheesy Puffs, 174
    Crawfish Bread, 77
    Crawfish Crostini, 78
    Crawfish Elegante, 79
    Crostini with Goat Cheese and Mushrooms, 143
    Farmer's Market Squares, 113
    Herbed Oyster Crackers, 191
    Holiday Cucumber Cups, 17
    Jack Quesadillas with Cranberry Pear Relish, 16
    Louisiana Crab Cakes with Sauce Ravigotte, 127
    Mexican Corn Bread Mini Muffins, 79
    Miniature Tomato Sandwiches, 128
    Monster Eyeballs, 161
    Olive Cheese Puffs, 16
    Open-Face Cucumber Sandwiches, 46
    Party Sandwiches, 47
    Shrimp Pastry Shells, 15
    Tiny Taco Tarts, 80
    Tomato Cups, 62

Apple
    Apple Slaw, 148
    Cambridge Club's Blueberry
      Apple Pie, 105
    Fresh Apple Cake, 155
    Fruit Salsa with Cinnamon-Sugar
      Crisps, 129
    Harvest Muffins, 145
    Winter Fruit Salad, 32

Artichokes
    Artichoke Bread, 130
    Marinated Artichoke Salad, 176
    Pasta Sauce Raphael, 52
    Shrimp and Grits with Artichokes, 53
    Warm Artichoke and Salsa Dip, 192

Asparagus
    Asparagus Party Rolls, 15
    Asparagus with White Wine Vinaigrette, 50
    Oriental Asparagus Salad, 116

Banana
    Banana Split Cake, 121
    Fourth of July Trifle, 121
    Fruit Pizza, 120
    Fruit Salsa with Cinnamon-Sugar Crisps, 129
    Winter Fruit Salad, 32

Beans
    Baked Black Olive Minestrone, 19
    Black Bean Wraps with Pico de Gallo, 54
    Black-Eyed Pea Dip, 18
    Creamy White Chicken Chili, 34
    Fall Bean Salad, 148
    Good Luck Salad, 18
    Green Bean Bundles, 193
    Green Bean Casserole, 177
    K.C. Baked Beans, 117
    Real Cajun Red Beans and Rice, 35
    Sweet 'n' Hot Green Beans and Carrots, 117

Beef. *See also* Ground Beef
    Baked Black Olive Minestrone, 19
    Beef Brisket, 119
    Beef Tenderloin with Mushrooms, 196
    London Grill, 151
    Pasta Salad with Steak, 132
    Steak Teriyaki, 119
    Strip Steak with Tomatoes and Olives, 135

Beverages. *See also* Punch
    Almond Tea, 126
    Brandy Smashers, 142
    Champagne Sorbet, 14
    Cinnamon Winter Cider, 190
    Electric Lemonade, 126
    Mexican Slush, 76
    Pineapple Margarita, 76
    Raspberry Lemonade Coolers, 112
    Vodka Snow, 14
    Watermelon Slushy, 112
    White Russian, 174

Blueberry
    Blueberry Barbecue Sauce, 180
    Blueberry Bread Pudding, 104
    Blueberry Salsa, 95
    Blueberry Sauce, 103
    Blueberry Sausage Breakfast Cake, 103
    Cambridge Club's Blueberry Apple Pie, 105
    Fourth of July Trifle, 121
    Fruit Pizza, 120
    Shuqualak Farms Blueberry Popsicles, 106

Breads. *See also* Muffins
    Chocolate Zucchini Bread, 146
    Cream Biscuits, 182
    Easy Cheddar Biscuits, 130

Breakfast/Brunch
Baked Peach French Toast, 104
Blueberry Sausage Breakfast Cake, 103
Christmas Morning Eggs, 197
Good Morning Pumpkin Pancakes, 162
Monkey Bread, 70

Broccoli
All-Time Favorite Broccoli Casserole, 151
Broccoli Sausage Pie, 20
Farmer's Market Squares, 113
Jalapeño Chicken, 85

Cakes
Chocolate Chip Pound Cake, 198
Chocolate Sheet Cake, 169
Easy King Cake, 40
Fresh Apple Cake, 155
Honey Bun Cake, 156
Lemonade Cake, 137
Mandarin Orange Cake, 137
Mardi Gras King Cake, 38
Pumpkin Pie Cake, 168
Strawberry Cake, 57
Triple-Decker Peanut Butter Cake, 90
White Sheet Cake, 169

Carrots
Baked Black Olive Minestrone, 19
Black Bean Wraps with Pico de Gallo, 54
Carrot Nut Sandwich Filling, 47
Farmer's Market Squares, 113
Harvest Muffins, 145
Pepper Jelly-Glazed Carrots, 33
Sweet 'n' Hot Green Beans and Carrots, 117

Catfish
Cajun Catfish with Strawberry Sauce, 51
Crispy Catfish with Homemade Tartar Sauce, 68

Cauliflower
Cauliflower au Gratin, 177
Farmer's Market Squares, 113

Cheddar Cheese
Awesome au Gratin Potatoes, 33
Baked Potato Casserole, 194
Derby Cheese Torta, 17
Easy Cheddar Biscuits, 130
Monster Eyeballs, 161
Olive Cheese Puffs, 16

Cheese. *See also* Cheddar Cheese
Artichoke Bread, 130
Blue Cheese Twice-Baked Potatoes, 164
Brown Sugar Brie, 142
Cheese Grits, 53

Cheezies, 63
Cocktail Cheesy Puffs, 174
Corn with Zucchini and Pepper Jack Cheese, 133
Crostini with Goat Cheese and Mushrooms, 143
Goat Cheese Polenta, 88
Hot Bacon and Swiss Dip, 32
Jack-O'-Lantern Cheeseburger Pie, 165
Knocchi, 51
Layered Crab Meat Spread, 31
Party Sandwiches, 47
Superior Grill's Chili con Queso, 144
Tomato Cups, 62

Chicken
Apricot-Glazed Chicken, 136
Barbecued Chicken Potpie, 154
Brown Rice Chicken Cranberry Salad, 193
Buttermilk Baked Chicken, 168
Chicken and Sausage Gumbo, 21
Chicken Bacon Bites with Apricot Sauce, 94
Chicken Mango Salad, 49
Chicken Spaghetti, 195
Creamy Chicken Lasagna, 167
Creamy White Chicken Chili, 34
Fairfield Market Chicken Salad, 64
Greek Chicken Kabobs, 101
Heavenly Chicken Casserole, 22
Jalapeño Chicken, 85
Skillet Pasta, 67
Strawn's Eat Shop Fried Chicken, 118

Chili
Creamy White Chicken Chili, 34
Venison Chili, 181

Chocolate
Andes Chocolate Mint Cookies, 199
Black Forest Brownies, 58
Caramel Chocolate Squares, 185
Chocolate Amaretto Cheesecake, 23
Chocolate Chip Pound Cake, 198
Chocolate Play Dough, 72
Chocolate Sheet Cake, 169
Chocolate Zucchini Bread, 146
Dirt Dessert, 70
"Everything but the Kitchen Sink" Bar Cookies, 156
German Chocolate Fondue, 26
Grand Chocolate Pie, 198
Mabry House White and Dark Chocolate Torte, 24
Oreo Balls, 40
Turtle Candy, 107

Cookies
Andes Chocolate Mint Cookies, 199
Candy Cane Snowballs, 199
Lemonade Cookies, 138
Soft Gingersnaps, 186

Cookies, Bar
Ambrosia Bars, 25
Black Forest Brownies, 58
Caramel Chocolate Squares, 185
"Everything but the Kitchen Sink"
    Bar Cookies, 156
Honey Bars, 107
Peach Pie Bars, 108

Corn
Corn Bread Casserole, 195
Corn Dip, 80
Corn Soufflé, 134
Corn with Zucchini and Pepper Jack Cheese, 133
Crawfish and Corn Soup, 81
Crawfish Boil, 86
Good Luck Salad, 18
Green Bean Casserole, 177
Mexican Corn Bread Mini Muffins, 79
Rice and Peach Salad, 97
Roasted Corn on the Cob, 118

Cornish Game Hens, Orange Honey-Glazed, 181

Crab Meat
Layered Crab Meat Spread, 31
Louisiana Crab Cakes with Sauce Ravigotte, 127
Marinated Crab Claws, 30

Cranberry
Brown Rice Chicken Cranberry Salad, 193
Cranberry and Sweet Potato Bake, 178
Cranberry Jezebel Sauce, 175
Cranberry Pear Relish, 16
Cranberry Raisin Bread Pudding, 184
Cranberry Salsa, 176
Mustard-Roasted Salmon with Cranberry Sauce, 197
Sugared Cranberries, 191

Crawfish
Cajun Pasta Salad, 83
Crawfish and Corn Soup, 81
Crawfish Boil, 86
Crawfish Bread, 77
Crawfish Crostini, 78
Crawfish Elegante, 79
Creamy Crawfish Pasta, 87

Cucumbers
Holiday Cucumber Cups, 17
Open-Face Cucumber Sandwiches, 46
Orzo and Shrimp Salad, 65
Yogurt and Cucumber Salad, 131

Desserts. *See also* Cakes; Cookies; Pies; Sauces, Sweet
Banana Split Cake, 121
Blueberry Bread Pudding, 104
Chocolate Amaretto Cheesecake, 23
Chocolate Play Dough, 72
Cranberry Raisin Bread Pudding, 184
Cream Cheese Squares, 89
Dinosaur Toes, 71
Dirt Dessert, 70
Four-Layer Lemon Delight, 42
Fourth of July Trifle, 121
Fruit Pizza, 120
German Chocolate Fondue, 26
Lemon Pull-Aparts, 55
Mabry House White and Dark Chocolate Torte, 24
Mexican Chew Bread, 89
Oreo Balls, 40
Shuqualak Farms Blueberry Popsicles, 106
Strawberry and Lemon Cream Roulade, 56
Stuffed Strawberries, 55
Superior Steakhouse's Krispy Kreme Bread
    Pudding, 170
Turtle Candy, 107
White Chocolate Macadamia Crème Brûlée, 41
White Chocolate Raspberry Tart, 120

Dips
Apple Dip, 144
Black-Eyed Pea Dip, 18
Corn Dip, 80
Hot Bacon and Swiss Dip, 32
Hot Onion Soufflé Dip, 192
Pumpkin Dip, 162
Roasted Butternut Squash Dip, 161
Superior Grill's Chili con Queso, 144
Warm Artichoke and Salsa Dip, 192

Duck
Duck Gumbo, 182
Walker's Ducks, 183

Eggplant Rolls in Tomato Sauce, Chianti's, 48

Fish. *See also* Catfish; Salmon
Baked Fish with Parmesan Sour Cream
    Sauce, 136

Frostings/Icings
Confectioners' Sugar Icing, 107, 156
Fudge Frosting, 169
Peanut Butter Frosting, 90
Pineapple Icing, 137
Strawberry Cream Cheese Frosting, 57

Fruits. *See also* Apple; Banana; Blueberry;
    Cranberry; Kiwifruit; Lemon; Mango;
    Orange; Peach; Pear; Pineapple; Pumpkin;
    Salads, Fruit; Strawberry
Chicken Mango Salad, 49
White Chocolate Raspberry Tart, 120

Grits
    Cheese Grits, 53
    Knocchi, 51

Ground Beef
    Beef Lombardi, 152
    Homemade Sloppy Joes, 66
    Jack-O'-Lantern Cheeseburger Pie, 165
    Mexican Corn Bread Mini Muffins, 79
    Mexican Lasagna, 84
    Natchitoches Meat Pies, 153

Gumbo
    Chicken and Sausage Gumbo, 21
    Duck Gumbo, 182

Ham
    Christmas Morning Eggs, 197
    Party Sandwiches, 47

Kiwifruit
    Fruit Pizza, 120
    Fruit Salsa with Cinnamon-Sugar Crisps, 129
    Fruity Spring Salad Mix, 115
    Winter Fruit Salad, 32

Leeks, Sweet-and-Sour, 19

Lemon
    Four-Layer Lemon Delight, 42
    Lemonade Cake, 137
    Lemon Dill New Potatoes, 65
    Lemon Pull-Aparts, 55
    Lemon Vanilla Sauce, 184
    Strawberry and Lemon Cream Roulade, 56

Mango
    Pineapple Mango Salsa, 114
    Strawberry Mango Salsa, 113

Muffins
    Harvest Muffins, 145
    Mexican Corn Bread Mini Muffins, 79

Mushrooms
    Beef Tenderloin with Mushrooms, 196
    Cajun Strata, 36
    Crostini with Goat Cheese and Mushrooms, 143

Nuts. *See* Pecans

Olives
    Baked Black Olive Minestrone, 19
    Farmer's Market Squares, 113
    Monster Eyeballs, 161
    Olive Cheese Puffs, 16
    Strip Steak with Tomatoes and Olives, 135

Orange
    Almond Mandarin Salad, 82
    Fruity Spring Salad Mix, 115
    Mandarin Orange Cake, 137
    Strawberry Orange Salad with Citrus Dressing, 49
    Winter Fruit Salad, 32

Pasta. *See also* Salads, Pasta
    Baked Black Olive Minestrone, 19
    Beef Lombardi, 152
    Chicken Mango Salad, 49
    Chicken Spaghetti, 195
    Creamy Chicken Lasagna, 167
    Creamy Crawfish Pasta, 87
    Skillet Pasta, 67

Peach
    Baked Peach French Toast, 104
    Peach Pie Bars, 108
    Pulled Pork with Peaches, 99
    Rice and Peach Salad, 97
    Salmon with Peach Jam, 102

Pear
    Cranberry Pear Relish, 16
    Pear and Blue Cheese Salad, 147

Peas
    Layered Green Salad, 63
    Rice and Peach Salad, 97
    Spring Pea Salad, 64

Pecans
    Carrot Nut Sandwich Filling, 47
    Peach Pie Bars, 108
    Sugared Pecans, 49

Peppers
    Chicken and Sausage Gumbo, 21
    Roasted Red Pepper Bisque, 150
    Shrimp Étouffée, 37
    Vegetable Couscous Salad, 131
    Vegetable Pies, 99

Pies
    Cambridge Club's Blueberry Apple Pie, 105
    Grand Chocolate Pie, 198
    Strawberry Daiquiri Pies, 138
    Streusel-Topped Pumpkin Pie, 185

Pineapple
    Banana Split Cake, 121
    Dinosaur Toes, 71
    Fruity Spring Salad Mix, 115
    Pineapple Icing, 137
    Pineapple Mango Salsa, 114
    Winter Fruit Salad, 32

Pork. *See also* Ham; Sausage
  Grilled Tenderloin with Blueberry Sauce, 180
  Honey Garlic Pork Tenderloin, 166
  Pork Shish Kabobs, 100
  Pulled Pork with Peaches, 99

Potatoes. *See also* Sweet Potatoes
  Awesome au Gratin Potatoes, 33
  Baked Potato Casserole, 194
  Blue Cheese Twice-Baked Potatoes, 164
  Crawfish Boil, 86
  Crisp Sweet Potato Wedges, 98
  Lemon Dill New Potatoes, 65
  New Potatoes on Rosemary Skewers, 97
  Ranch French Fries, 66
  Roasted Rosemary Potato Salad, 149
  Squash Potato Casserole, 165

Poultry. *See* Chicken; Turkey

Pumpkin
  Good Morning Pumpkin Pancakes, 162
  Pumpkin Dip, 162
  Pumpkin Pie Cake, 168
  Streusel-Topped Pumpkin Pie, 185

Punch
  Autumn Hot Cranberry Citrus Punch, 160
  Best Tea Punch, 46
  Coffee Punch, 30
  Peach Party Punch, 62
  Peppermint Punch, 190
  Witches' Brew, 160

Rice
  Brown Rice Chicken Cranberry Salad, 193
  Heavenly Chicken Casserole, 22
  Jambalaya, 37
  Real Cajun Red Beans and Rice, 35
  Rice and Peach Salad, 97

Salad Dressings
  Balsamic Dressing, 82
  Balsamic Italian Dressing, 131
  Herbed Dressing, 83
  Raspberry Vinaigrette, 147
  Sweet Hot Vinaigrette, 115
  Sweet Slaw Vinaigrette, 148
  Tarragon Vinaigrette, 96
  White Wine Vinaigrette, 50

Salads, Fruit
  Almond Mandarin Salad, 82
  Apple Slaw, 148
  Fruity Spring Salad Mix, 115
  Pear and Blue Cheese Salad, 147
  Rice and Peach Salad, 97

Strawberry Orange Salad with Citrus Dressing, 49
Winter Fruit Salad, 32

Salads, Main Dish
  Brown Rice Chicken Cranberry Salad, 193
  Cajun Pasta Salad, 83
  Chicken Mango Salad, 49
  Fairfield Market Chicken Salad, 64
  Orzo and Shrimp Salad, 65
  Pasta Salad with Steak, 132

Salads, Pasta
  Cajun Pasta Salad, 83
  Pasta Salad with Steak, 132

Salads, Vegetable
  Almond Mandarin Salad, 82
  Apple Slaw, 148
  Asian Slaw, 96
  Asparagus with White Wine Vinaigrette, 50
  Easy Coleslaw, 116
  Fall Bean Salad, 148
  Good Luck Salad, 18
  Green Salad with Tarragon Vinaigrette, 96
  Layered Green Salad, 63
  Marinated Artichoke Salad, 176
  Oriental Asparagus Salad, 116
  Roasted Rosemary Potato Salad, 149
  Spring Pea Salad, 64
  Vegetable Couscous Salad, 131
  Yogurt and Cucumber Salad, 131

Salmon
  Mustard-Roasted Salmon with Cranberry Sauce, 197
  Salmon with Peach Jam, 102

Salsas
  Blueberry Salsa, 95
  Cranberry Salsa, 176
  Fruit Salsa with Cinnamon-Sugar Crisps, 129
  Pineapple Mango Salsa, 114
  Strawberry Mango Salsa, 113

Sauces, Savory
  Apricot Dipping Sauce, 94
  Blueberry Barbecue Sauce, 180
  Homemade Tartar Sauce, 68
  Pasta Sauce Raphael, 52
  Sauce Ravigotte, 127
  Simple Tomato Sauce, 48
  Strawberry Sauce, 51
  White Sauce, 53

Sauces, Sweet
  Blueberry Sauce, 103
  Jack Daniel's Ice Cream Sauce, 122
  Lemon Vanilla Sauce, 184

Sausage
Blueberry Sausage Breakfast Cake, 103
Broccoli Sausage Pie, 20
Cajun Strata, 36
Chicken and Sausage Gumbo, 21
Duck Gumbo, 182
Jambalaya, 37
Monster Eyeballs, 161
Natchitoches Meat Pies, 153
Real Cajun Red Beans and Rice, 35
Sausage-Stuffed Acorn Squash, 164
Torta Rustica, 134

Seafood. *See* Crab Meat; Crawfish; Fish; Shrimp

Shrimp
Barbecued Shrimp, 67
Chipotle Prawns with Goat Cheese Polenta, 88
Dijon Shrimp, 102
Jambalaya, 37
Orzo and Shrimp Salad, 65
Shrimp and Grits with Artichokes, 53
Shrimp Étouffée, 37
Shrimp Pastry Shells, 15

Side Dishes. *See also* Grits; Rice
Corn Bread Casserole, 195
Goat Cheese Polenta, 88
Southern Corn Bread Dressing and Gravy, 179

Soups. *See also* Chili; Gumbo
Baked Black Olive Minestrone, 19
Butternut Squash Bisque, 163
Crawfish and Corn Soup, 81
Roasted Red Pepper Bisque, 150

Spinach
Black Bean Wraps with Pico de Gallo, 54
Derby Cheese Torta, 17

Spreads
Carrot Nut Sandwich Filling, 47
Derby Cheese Torta, 17
Layered Crab Meat Spread, 31
Red Pesto, 31

Squash
Baked Black Olive Minestrone, 19
Butternut Squash Bisque, 163
Chocolate Zucchini Bread, 146
Corn with Zucchini and Pepper Jack Cheese, 133
Roasted Butternut Squash Dip, 161
Sausage-Stuffed Acorn Squash, 164
Squash Potato Casserole, 165
Vegetable Pies, 99

Strawberry
Fourth of July Trifle, 121
Fruit Pizza, 120
Fruit Salsa with Cinnamon-Sugar Crisps, 129
Strawberry and Lemon Cream Roulade, 56
Strawberry Cake, 57
Strawberry Mango Salsa, 113
Strawberry Orange Salad with Citrus Dressing, 49
Strawberry Sauce, 51
Stuffed Strawberries, 55

Sweet Potatoes
Cranberry and Sweet Potato Bake, 178
Superior Steakhouse's Whipped Sweet
    Potatoes, 178

Tomatoes
Baked Black Olive Minestrone, 19
Corn Dip, 80
Farmer's Market Squares, 113
Good Luck Salad, 18
Herbed Tomatoes, 114
Miniature Tomato Sandwiches, 128
Orzo and Shrimp Salad, 65
Pasta Sauce Raphael, 52
Pico de Gallo, 54
Simple Tomato Sauce, 48
Strip Steak with Tomatoes and Olives, 135
Tomato Cups, 62
Torta Rustica, 134
Vegetable Couscous Salad, 131
Vegetable Pies, 99

Turkey
Jack Quesadillas with Cranberry Pear Relish, 16

Turnip Greens Casserole, 34

Vegetables. *See* Artichokes; Asparagus; Beans;
    Broccoli; Carrots; Cauliflower; Corn;
    Cucumbers; Eggplant; Leeks; Mushrooms;
    Olives; Peas; Peppers; Potatoes;
    Salads, Vegetable; Spinach; Squash;
    Tomatoes; Turnip Greens

Venison Chili, 181

$\mathcal{M}$ARDI GRAS TO MISTLETOE

Junior League of Shreveport-Bossier, Inc.
520 Olive Street, Suite B204
Shreveport, Louisiana 71104
318-221-6144
www.jlsb.org

Name
_____

Street Address
_____

City _____ State _____ Zip _____

Telephone
_____

Your Order	Qty	Total
Mardi Gras to Mistletoe at $26.95 per book		$
Revel at $19.95 per book		$
Louisiana residents add 8.6% sales tax		$
Shipping and handling at $6.00 for first book; $1.00 for each additional book shipped to the same address		$
Total		$

Payment Method: [   ] MasterCard   [   ] VISA
                  [   ] Check payable to Junior League of Shreveport-Bossier, Inc.

_____
Account Number   Expiration Date

_____
Signature

Photocopies will be accepted.